FIG-Forth 'Knight Rider' LEDS with our 1802 on the Lattice ICE 8k board.

FIG-Forth Manual
C-H Ting

plus **running Fig-Forth Code
on 1802 IP in Lattice FPGA as test**

Part of the Forth eBook Series

Juergen Pintaske – ExMark – June 2020

**Thanks to Steve Teal and Scott Baker for the 1802s
and a Lattice ICE 8k Board flashed to test FIG-Forth**

The current Forth Bookshelf can be found at
https://www.amazon.co.uk/Juergen-Pintaske/e/B00N8HVEZM

All available as eBook – most of them as Print Book as well. Special thanks to Michael Kalus, Dirk Bruehl, Steve Teal and many others

CONTENTS

Link to additional information at Forth-eV.de:
https://wiki.forth-ev.de/doku.php/projects:fig-forth-1802-fpga:start

Link to Steve Teal's github with the 1802 VHDL designed for this project
https://github.com/Steve-Teal/1802-pico-basic

File: FIG-Forth_v10e 07/06/2020

figFORTH REFUSES TO DIE   (note from 1989)

PREFACE FOR THE SECOND EDITION

The first edition of Systems Guide to figForth was published almost ten years ago. Forth has made significant changes, and perhaps some improvements since. The figForth Model was supposedly replaced by Forth-78, Forth-79, and Forth-83 Standards, at least that is the impressions Forth experts wanted us to believe. FigForth should have been laid to rest long, long ago. In its place, there are many better, larger, and more comprehensive Forth implementations available from many vendors, and also in the public domain. Why would anybody want to use this old fashioned figForth?

The fact remains that figForth is still very popular. Among all the publications sold by the Forth Interest Group over the years, Bill Ragsdale's figForth Installation Manual has always been the most demanded document. I have also decided many times to quit reprinting this book, but Roy Martens of the Mountain View Press just keeps on ordering them. There must be some magic behind figForth, keeping it alive despite its age, the lack of support, and its deficiency in tools for serious program development.

However, there are many advantages in figForth which make it useful to many programmers and new students of Forth. Here is a list:

1. Consistency. It is a single model implemented uniformly on many microprocessors. Many implementations are readily available in assembly listings.
2. Well factored kernel. Less than 50 words are machine dependent. All other words are defined in high level. It is easily portable to other microprocessors and operating systems.
3. The source code is in regular assembly, which can be understood by most programmers. Most other Forth systems are generated through meta compilation, and the source code are only available in Forth. The Forth source listing is difficult for Forth programmer to understand, let alone non-Forth programmers.
4. Simplicity. It provides only the functionality to be self-supporting. Lacking of extensive and complicated utility makes it easier to study and comprehend.

Generally, it is impossible to study and understand a commercial Forth system. The source code is not available in most cases. Where the source code is provided, it is too complicated to be dissected and to be put back together again. For people who are curious about how Forth really ticks, figForth is the only Forth system that an average person can understand in a couple of weeks. It is also easy to port figForth to a virgin computer un-adulterated by a prior Forth implementation. This I found ten years ago, and I think it is still true today. We have no valid alternative in teaching and learning Forth besides this old figForth.

The original manuscript of this book was written using the ED line editor under the RT-11 operating system on a DEC LSI-11 microcomputer. That was the desk top publishing system of the day. The text was first entered in upper case only, because the old ADM terminal I used did not have lower case characters. It was painfully converted to lower case and eventually printed out using a letter quality printer. However, lines were too long to fit on a page. The printing was done using 1/10" characters with 1/16" spacings, and the characters tended to rub elbows with one another. Lines were doubly spaced so that it gave the reader the illusion of a thick manual with substance. The result was an eye-sore, whether I admitted it or not.

In spite of the poor condition of this book, I often ran into people who complimented me for it. Many of them mentioned that it leads them to the understanding of the figForth Model and the appreciation of Forth as a programming language. Now, since I have much better tools for desk top publishing, it is time to give this book a facelift so that it does some justice to the figForth Model and its faithful users.

Only cosmetic touches are made in this revision. As I re-visited the chapters, I found most of the discussions are still useful for people wanted to fully understand Forth. After ten years, we have many more books on Forth. However, none of them tried to present Forth in the bottom-up and inside-out fashion this book did. Besides, the discussions on syntax of Forth, the detailed implementation of Forth editor and assemblers are not covered in available Forth literature.

I like to thank Bill Ragsdale, Kim Harris, Bob Smith, John James, John Cassidy, and the members of the Forth Implementation Team to provide the figForth Model and implementations and their efforts in my enlightenment. I am also indebted to Kevin Appert in helping me move the manuscript from the RT-11 system into MS-DOS so that I had free access to the texts again.

C. H. Ting
San Mateo, California
April 1989

PREFACE TO THE FIRST EDITION

Forth was developed by Charles Moore in the 1960's. It took the final form as we now know it in 1969, when Mr. Moore was at the National Radio Astronomy Observatory, Charlottesville, Va. It was created out of his dissatisfaction with available programming tools, especially for instrumentation control and automation. Distribution of his work to other observatories has made Forth the standard language for observatory automation. Mr. Moore and several associates formed FORTH, Inc. in 1973, for the purpose of licensing and support of the Forth operating system and programming language, and to supply application software to meet customers' unique requirements.

Forth Interest Group was formed in 1978 by a group of Forth programmer in Northern California. It is a non-profit organization. Its purpose is to encourage the use of Forth language by the interchange of ideas through seminars and publications. It organized a Forth Implementation Team in 1978 to develop Forth operating systems for popular microprocessors from a common language model, now known as figForth. In early 1979, the Forth Implementation Team published six assembly listings of figForth for 8080, 6800, 6502, PDP-11, 9900, and PACE at $10.00 each. The quality and availability of these listings, which are placed in the public domain, made figForth the most popular dialect in Forth.

Most of the published materials on Forth are manuals which teach how to use a particularly Forth implementation on a particular computer. Very few deal with the inner mechanisms on how the Forth system operates which is essential to the understanding and effective utilization of the Forth language. My intention here is to describe how the Forth system does all these wonderful things no other language can. With a deeper understanding of the inner mechanism, a user can have a better appreciation of many unique features which make Forth such a powerful programming tool.

Among other things, documentation on Forth is very difficult to read and to comprehend because Forth definitions are short and their numbers are many. The definitions are very hard to arrange in a logical order to promote better or easier understanding. For example, the glossary is arranged alphabetically, which is great for reference purposes. If you know which definition you are looking for, you can find it very conveniently in the glossary, but how a definition is related to others and how it is to be used are not easy to find. The source codes, coded in Forth, are also difficult to comprehend because the definitions are ordered from bottom up, i.e., low-level definitions must precede the higher level definitions using the low-level definitions. I will not mention the problems in reading codes written with postfix notations. These are problems for which Forth is often criticized. A book on the systems aspect in the figForth Model can help programmers to climb the learning curve and ease somewhat the growing pain in learning this very strange language.

In this book, I will attempt to explain the operation of figForth system in a systematic fashion. The top level Forth definitions related to the system operations are treated in logical sequences. Most of these definitions are defined in terms of other predefined Forth definitions; therefore, it is required that the reader has some basic knowledge of the elements contained in the Forth language, such as the dictionary, the data stack, and the return stack. However, the Forth language is structured and modular, so that the logical contents of a definition are not difficult to grasp if the functions of all the low-level definitions involved are clearly stated.

Because of the modular structures inherent in the Forth language, the definition of a Forth word itself is a fine vehicle to convey its function. In fact, the definition can be used in lieu of a flow chart. In our discussions, Forth definitions are laid out in a vertical format. The component definitions are written in a column on the left hand, side of a page, and the comments and explanations are in columns toward the right-hand side. When a group of words of very close relationship (a phrase) appears, it is often displayed in one line to save space.

Many Forth words are defined in machine codes. They are called code definitions or primitive definitions and they form the body of what is called the "virtual Forth machine ". These definitions are used to convert a particular CPU into a Forth computer. The detailed contents of these words cannot be discussed without resorting to the assembly language of the host CPU, and we shall avoid their discussion as much as possible. In the cases, where it is absolutely necessary to use them in order to clarify how the system functions, the figForth PDP-11 codes will be used because the PDP-11 instruction set is very close to what is required optimally to implement a virtual Forth computer.

The detailed definitions of Forth words will strictly adhere to those defined in the figForth model as presented in the figForth Installation Manual. This model is the most complete and consistent documentation defining a Forth language system which has been implemented on a host of microcomputers.

The Forth operating system written in Forth provides the best examples for the serious students to learn the Forth language. Most of the programming tools provided by the Forth system were developed to code the Forth system itself. By going through the Forth system carefully, a Forth user can learn most programming techniques supported by the Forth language for his own use.

In Chapter 1, I try to lay down the formal definition of Forth as a programming language. It was completed only very recently, after all other chapters were done. Some terms used in Chapter 1 are not quite consistent with those used in the later chapters. The terms 'word', 'definition', and 'instruction' are used interchangeably in later chapters are differentiated in Chapter 1. Chapter 2 is an overview of the figForth operating system.

In the rest of the book, each chapter will dwell on a particular topic in the figForth system. The more important definitions at the highest level, which the user will use most often are discussed first to give an overall view of the tasks involved. The low-level definitions or utility definitions used by the high-level definitions are then discussed in detail to complete the entire picture. Descriptive comments are given for the low-level definitions when they appear in a high-level definition before they are completely defined. Therefore, it will be helpful to re-read a chapter so that the knowledge gained by studying the utility definitions can further illuminate the high-level definition outlining the task involved.

Special thanks are due to William F. Ragsdale, who authored the figForth Installation Manual and guides the Forth Interest Group from its inception, to John S. James, who developed the PDP-11 figForth and the PDP-11 Assembler, and to John Cassady, who developed the 8080 figForth and the 8080 Assembler. Thanks are also due to Robert Downs, Anson Averrell, Alice Ferrish and Albert Ting, who kindly gave me long lists of corrections and made many helpful suggestions on the manuscript.

C. H. Ting
San Mateo, Ca.
May, 1981.

SYSTEMS GUIDE TO figFORTH

Chapter 1. LANGUAGE DEFINITION OF FORTH

Forth was developed as a programming tool to solve real time control problems. It has never been formally defined as a programming language. I think Forth is mature enough now that it can be defined very rigorously. The wide-spread use of this powerful language requires that a common base should be established to facilitate the exchange of programs and ideas in a standardized language form. The recent publication of Forth-79 Standard clearly reflects this necessity. To define Forth as a programming language also helps us to focus our attention on the basic characteristics of Forth and to understand it more fully.

In this Chapter, I will present the definition of Forth in the Backus Normal Form (BNF) notation. The basic syntax is presented in Table 1, in which the focal point is the definition of 'word'. Some detailed clarifications on colon definitions and defining words are worked out in Tables 2 to 4. Explanatory notes are arranged by sections to highlight some problems not readily expressed in the formal definitions.

TABLE 1. LANGUAGE DEFINITION OF FORTH

<character> ::= <ASCII code>

<delimiting character> ::= NUL | CR | SP | <designated character>

<delimiter> ::= <delimiting character> |

<delimiting character><delimiter>

<word> ::= <instruction> | <number> | <string>

<string> ::= <character> | <character><string>

<number> ::= <integer> | -<integer>

<integer> ::= <digit> | <digit><integer>

<digit> ::= 0 | 1 | 2 | ... | 9 | A | B | ... | <base-1>

<instruction> ::= <standard instruction> | <user instruction>

<standard instruction> ::= <nucleus instruction> |

<interpreter instruction> |

<compiler instruction> | <device instruction>

<user instruction> ::= <colon instruction> | <code instruction> |

<constant> | <variable> | <vocabulary>

1.1. PROGRAMMING LANGUAGE

A programming language is a set of symbols with rules (syntax) of combining them to specify execution procedures to a computer. A programming language is used primarily to instruct a computer to perform specific functions. However, it can also be used by programmers to document and to communicate problem solving procedures. The most essential ingredients of a programming language are therefore the symbols it employs for expressions and the syntax rules of combining the symbols for man-to-machine and man-to-man communications.

Forth uses the full set of ASCII characters as symbols. Most programming languages use subsets of ASCII characters, including only numerals, upper-case alphabets, and some punctuation characters. Use of punctuation characters differs significantly from language to language. Non-printable characters are generally reserved exclusively for the system and are not available for language usage. In employing the full ASCII set of characters, Forth thus allows the programmer a much wider range of usable symbols to name objects. On the other hand, the prolific use of punctuation characters in Forth makes comprehension very difficult by uninitiated programmers.

Only five of the ASCII characters are used by Forth for special system functions and are not for programming usage: NUL (ASCII 0), BS (ASCII 7), RUB (ASCII 127), CR (ASCII 13), and SP (ASCII 32). BS and RUB are used to nullify the previously entered character. They are used at the keyboard interactively to correct typing errors. NUL, CR, and SP are delimiting characters to separate groups of characters to form words. All other characters can be freely used to form words and are used the same way. Non-printable characters are treated the same as printable characters. Because non-printable characters are difficult to document and to display, their usage is discouraged in normal Forth programming practice. However, the non-printable characters are very useful in maintaining a secured system.

1.2. WORDS

Words are the basic syntactical units in Forth. A word is a group of characters separated from other words by delimiting characters. With the exception of NUL, CR, SP, BS and RUB, any ASCII character may be part of a word. Certain words for string processing may specify a regular character as the delimiting character for the string immediately following it, in order to override the delimiting effect of SP. However, the delimiting effect of CR and NUL cannot be overriden.

The usage of 'word' in Forth literature is very confusing because many quite different concepts are associated with it. Without sorting out these different aspects of 'word' into independently identifiable entities, it is impossible to arrive at a satisfactory description of Foth language. Here 'word' is defined as a syntactical unit in the language, simply a group of characters separated from other words by delimiting characters. Semantically (which concerns the meaning of words), a word in Forth can be only one of three things: a string, an instruction, or a number.

A Forth program is thus simply a list of words. When this list of words is given to a computer with a Forth operating system loaded in, the computer will be able to execute or interpret this list of words and perform functions as specified by this list. The functions may include compilation of new words into the system to perform complicated functions not implemented in the original Forth operating system.

A string is merely a group of characters to be processed by the Forth computer. To be processed correctly, a string must be preceded by an instruction which specifies exactly how this string is to be processed. The string instruction may even specify a regular character as the delimiting character for the following string to override the effect of SP. It is often appropriate to consider the string to be an integral part of the preceding instruction. However, this association would disturb the uniform and simple syntax rule in Forth and it is better to consider strings as independent objects in the language.

String processing is a major component in the Forth operating system because Forth is an interpretive language. Strings are needed to supply names for new instructions, to insert comments into source text for documentation, and to produce messages at run-time to facilitate the human interface. The resident Forth instructions for string processing are all available to programmers for string manipulations.

A number is a string which causes the Forth computer to push a piece of data onto the data stack. Characters used in a number must belong to a subset of ASCII characters--the numerals. The total number of numerals in this subset is equal to a 'base' value specified by the programmer. This subset starts from 0 and goes up to 9. If the 'base' value is larger than 10, the upper-case alphabets are used in their natural sequence. Any reasonable 'base' value can be specified and modified at run-time by the programmer. However, a very large base value causes excessive overlapping between numbers and instructions, and a 'reasonable base value' must avoid this conflict in semantic interpretation.

A number may have a leading '-' sign to designate data of negative value. Certain punctuation characters such as '.' are also allowed in numbers depending upon the particular Forth operating system.

The internal representation of numbers inside the Forth computer depends upon implementation. The most common format is a 16-bit integer number. Numbers are put on the data stack to be processed. The interpretation of a number depends entirely on the instruction which uses the number. A number may be used to represent a true-or-false flag, a 7-bit ASCII character, an 8-bit byte, a 16-bit signed or unsigned integer, a 16-bit address, etc. Two consecutive numbers may be used as a 32-bit signed or unsigned double integer, or a floating-point number.

Forth is not a typed language in which numerical data type must be declared and checked during compilation. Numbers are loaded on the data stack where all numbers are represented and treated identically. Instructions using the numbers on stack will take whatever they need for processing and push their results back on the stack. It is the responsibility of the programmer to put the correct data on the stack and use the correct instructions to retrieve them. Non-discriminating use of numbers on stack might seem to be a major source of errors in using Forth for programming. In practice, the use of stack greatly ease the debugging process in which individual instructions can be thoroughly exercised to spot any discrepancies in stack manipulation. The most important advantage gained in the uniform usage of data stored on data stack is that the instructions built this way are essentially context-free and can be repeatedly called in different environments to perform the same task.

Numbers and strings are objects or nouns in a programming language. Typed and named numbers in a program provide vital clues to the functions and the structures in a program. The explicitly defined objects or nouns make statements in a program easy to comprehend. The implicit use of data objects stored on the data stack makes Forth programs very tight and efficient. At the same time, statements in a program deprived of nouns are difficult to understand. For this reason, the most important task in documenting a Forth program is to specify the stack effects of the instructions, indicating what types of data are retrieved from the stack and what types of data are left on the stack upon exit.

1.3. STANDARD INSTRUCTIONS

In a Forth computer, an instruction is best defined as "a named, linked, memory resident, and executable entity which can be called and executed interactively". The entire linked list of instructions in the computer memory is called a dictionary. Instructions are known to the programmer by their ASCII names. The names of the instructions in a Forth computer are words that a programmer can use either to execute the instruction interactively or to build (compile) new instructions to solve his programming problem.

In Forth literature, instructions are called 'words', 'definitions', or 'word definitions'. The reason that I choose to called them 'instructions' is to emphasize the fact that an instruction given to the Forth computer causes immediate actions performed by the computer. The instructions in the dictionary are an instruction set of the Forth virtual computer, in the same sense as the instruction set of a real CPU. The difference is that the Forth instructions can be executed directly and the Forth instructions are accessed by their ASCII names. Therefore, Forth can be considered as a high level assembly language with an open instruction set for interactive programming and testing. The name 'instruction' conveys more precisely the characteristics of a Forth instruction than 'word' or 'definition' and leaves 'word' to mean exclusively a syntactical unit in the language definition.

An instruction set is the heart of a computer as well as of a language. In all conventional programming languages, the instruction set is immutable and limited in number and in scope. Programmers must circumvent the shortcomings of a language by writing programs to perform tasks that the native instruction set is not capable of. The instruction set in a Forth computer provides a basis or a skeleton from which a more sophisticated instruction set can be built and optimized to solve a particular problem.

Because the instruction set in Forth can be easily extended by the user, it is rather difficult to define precisely the minimum instruction set a Forth computer ought to have. The general requirement is that the minimum set should provide an environment in which typical programming problems can be solved conveniently. Forth-79 Standard suggested such a minimum instruction set as summarized in Table 2. The instructions provided by the operating system are called standard instructions, and are divided into nucleus instructions, interpreter instructions, compiler instructions, and device instructions.

TABLE 2. STANDARD INSTRUCTIONS

The list of standard instructions is basically that in Forth-79 Standard. Minor changes are made to conform to the instruction set used in the fig-Forth Model.

<nucleus instruction> ::=

```
| ! | * | */ | */MOD | + | +! | - | -DUP | / | /MOD |
| 0< | 0= | 0> | 1+ | 1- | 2+ | 2- | < | = | > | >R |
| @ |ABS | AND | C! | C@ | CMOVE | D+ | D< | DMINUS |
| DROP | DUP | EXECUTE | EXIT | FILL | MAX | MIN | MOD | MOVE |
| NOT | OR | OVER | R> | R | ROT | SWAP | U* | U/ | U< | XOR |
```

<interpreter instruction> ::=

```
| # | #> | #S | ' | ( | -TRAILING | . | <# | IN | ? | ABORT |
| BASE | BLK | CONTEXT | COUNT | CURRENT | DECIMAL | EXPECT |
| FIND | FORTH | HERE | HOLD | NUMBER | PAD | QUERY | QUIT |
| SIGN | SPACE | SPACES | TYPE | U. | WORD |
```

<compiler instruction> ::=

```
| +LOOP | , | ." | : | ; | ALLOT | BEGIN| COMPILE |
| CONSTANT | CREATE | DEFINITIONS | DO | DOES> | ELSE | ENDIF |
| FORGET | I | IF | IMMEDIATE | J | LEAVE | LITERAL | LOOP |
| REPEAT | STATE | UNTIL | VARIABLE | VOCABULARY | WHILE | [ |
| [COMPILE] | ] |
```

<device instruction> ::=

```
| BLOCK | BUFFER | CR | EMIT | EMPTY-BUFFERS |
| FLUSH | KEY | LIST | LOAD | SCR | UPDATE |
```

1.4. USER INSTRUCTIONS

Instructions created by a user are called user instructions. There are several classes of user instructions depending upon how they are created. High level instructions are called colon instructions because they are generated by the special instruction ':'. Low level instructions containing machine codes of the host CPU are called code instructions because they are generated by the instruction CODE. Other user instructions include constants, variables, and vocabularies.

Instructions are verbs in Forth language. They are commands given to the computer for execution. Instructions cause the computer to modify memory cells, to move data from one location to the other. Some instructions modify the size and the contents of the data stack. Implicitly using objects on the data stack eliminates many nouns in Forth programs. It is not uncommon to have lines of Forth text without a single noun. The verbs-only Forth text earns it the reputation of a 'write-only' language.

Forth is an interpretive language. Instructions given to the computer are generally executed immediately by the interpreter, which can be thought as the operating system in the Forth computer. This interpreter is called text interpreter or outer interpreter. A word given to the Forth computer is first parsed out of the input stream, and the text interpreter searches the dictionary for an instruction with the same name as the word given. If an instruction with a matching name is found, it is executed by the text interpreter. The text interpreter also performs the tasks of compiling new user instructions into the dictionary. The process of compiling new instructions is very much different from interpreting existing instructions. The text interpreter switches its mode of operation from interpretation to compilation by a group of special instructions called defining instructions, which perform the functions of language compilers in conventional computers.

Syntax of these defining instructions are more complicated than the normal Forth syntax because of the special conditions required of the compilation of different types of user instructions. The syntax of the defining instructions provided by a standard Forth operating system is summarized in Table 3. The most important defining instruction is the ':' or colon instruction. To define colon instructions satisfactorily, a new entity structure must be introduced. This concept and many other aspects involving defining instructions are discussed in the following subsections.

TABLE 3. USER INSTRUCTIONS

The statement in paranthesis is defined according to the Forth syntax.

COLON INSTRUCTION

```
<colon instruction> ::=
    <structure list>
  ( : <colon instruction> <structure list> ; )
```

\<structure list\> ::=
    \<structure\>\<delimiter\> |
    \<structure\>\<delimiter\>\<structure list\>

\<structure\> ::=
    \<word\> | \<if-else-then\> |
    \<begin-until\> | \<begin-while-repeat\> |
    \<do-loop\>

\<if-else-then\> ::=
    IF\<delimiter\>\<structure list
    \>THEN | IF\<delimiter\>\<structure
    list\>ELSE\<delimiter\>\<structure list\>THEN

\<begin-until\> ::= BEGIN\<delimiter\>
    \<structure list\>UNTIL

\<begin-while-repeat\> ::=
    BEGIN\<delimiter\>\<structure
    list\>WHILE\<delimiter\>\<structure list\>REPEAT

\<do-loop structure\> ::=
    \<structure\> | I | J | LEAVE

\<do-loop structure list\> ::=
    \<do-loop structure\>\<delimiter\> |

**\<do-loop structure\>\<delimiter\>\<do-loop
    structure list\>**

\<do-loop\> ::=
    DO\<delimiter\>\<do-loop structure list\>LOOP |
    DO\<delimiter\>\<do-loop structure list\>+LOOP

CODE INSTRUCTION

\<code instruction\> ::=
    \<assembly code list\>
   (CODE \<code instruction\> \<assembly code list\>)

```
<assembly code list> ::=
    <assembly code><delimiter> |
    <assembly code><delimiter><assembly code list>

<assembly code> ::=
    <number><delimiter>, | <number><delimiter>C,
```

CONSTANT INSTRUCTION

```
<constant> ::=
    <number>
    ( <number> CONSTANT <constant> )
```

VARIABLE INSTRUCTION

```
<variable> ::=
    <address>
    ( VARIABLE <variable> )

<address> ::=
    <integer>
```

VOCABULARY INSTRUCTION

```
<context vocabulary> ::=
    <vocabulary>
    ( VOCABULARY <vocabulary> )
```

1.5. Structures and Colon Instructions

Words are the basic syntactical units in Forth language. During run-time execution, each word has only one entry point and one exit point. After a word is processed by the interpreter, control returns to the text interpreter to process the next word consecutively. Compilation allows certain words to be executed repeatedly or to be skipped selectively at run-time. A set of instructions, equivalent to compiler directives in conventional programming languages, are used to build small modules to take care of these exceptional cases. These modules are called structures.

A structure is a list of words bounded by a pair of special compiler instructions, such as IF-THEN, BEGIN-UNTIL, or DO-LOOP. A structure, similar to an instruction, has only one entry point and one exit point. Within a structure, however, instruction or word sequence can be conditionally skipped or selectively repeated at run-time. Structures do not have names and they cannot be executed outside of the colon instruction in which it is defined. However, a structure can be given a name and be defined as a new user instruction. Structures can be nested, but two structures cannot overlap each other. This would violate the one-entry-one-exit rule for a structure.

Structure is the extension of a word. A structure should be considered as an integral entity like a word inside a colon instruction. Words and structures are the building blocks to create new user instructions at a higher level of program construct. Programming in Forth is progressively creating new instructions from low level to high level. All the instructions created at low levels are available to build new and more powerful instructions. The resulting instruction set then becomes the solution to the programming problem. This programming process contains naturally all the ingredients of the much touted structured programming in software engineering.

Using the definition of structures, the precise definition of a colon instruction is then a named, executable entity equivalent to a list of structures. When a colon instruction is invoked by the interpreter, the list of structures is executed in the order the structures were laid out in the colon instruction.

When a colon instruction is being compiled, words appearing on the list of structures are compiled into the body of the colon instruction as execution addresses. Thus, a colon instruction is similar to a list of subroutine calls in conventional programming languages. However, only the addresses of the called subroutines are compiled into the colon instruction because the CALL statement is implicit. Parameters are passed on the data stack and the argument list is eliminated also. Therefore, the memory overhead for a subroutine call is reduced to a bare minimum of two bytes in Forth. This justifies the claim that equivalent programs written in Forth are shorter than those written in assembly language.

Compiler instructions setting up the structures are not directly compiled into the body of colon instructions. Instead, they set up various mechanisms such as conditional tests and branch addresses in the compiled codes so that execution sequence can be directed correctly at run-time. The detailed codes that are compiled are implementation dependent.

1.6. Code Instructions

Colon instruction allows a user to extend the Forth system at a high level. Programs developed using only colon instructions are very tight and memory efficient. These programs are also transportable between different host computers because of the buffering of the Forth virtual computer. Nevertheless, there is an overhead in execution speed in using colon instructions. Colon instructions are often nested for many levels and the interpreter must go through these nested levels to find executable codes which are defined as code instructions. Typically, the nesting and unnesting of colon instructions (calling and returning) cost about 20% to 30% of execution time. If this execution overhead is too much to be tolerated in a time-critical situation, instructions can be coded in machine codes which will then be executed at the full machine speed. Instructions of this type are created by the CODE instruction, which is equivalent to a machine code assembler in conventional computer systems.

Machine code representation depends on the host computer. Each CPU has its own machine instruction set with its particular code format. The only universal machine code presentation is by numbers. To define code instructions in a generalized form suitable for any host computer, only two special compiler instructions, ',' (comma), and 'C,' are needed. C, takes a byte integer and compiles it to the body of the code instruction under construction, and ',' takes a 16-bit integer from the data stack and compiles it to the body of the code instruction. An assembly step is thus a number followed by 'C,' or ','. The body of a code instruction is a list of numbers representing a sequence of machine codes. As the code instruction is invoked by the interpreter, this sequence of machine codes will be executed by the host CPU.

Advanced Forth assemblers have been developed for almost all computers commercially available based on this simple syntax. Most Forth assemblers use names of assembly mnemonics to define a set of assembler instructions which facilitates coding and documenting of the code instructions. The detailed discussion of these advanced instructions is outside the scope of this Chapter. Two typical Forth assembler are discussed in Chapter 14.

1.7. Constants, Variables, and Vocabulary

The defining instructions CONSTANT and VARIABLE are used to introduce named numbers and named memory addresses to the Forth system, respectively. After a constant is defined, when the text interpreter encounters its name, the assigned value of this constant is pushed on the data stack. When the interpreter finds the name of a predefined variable, the address of this variable is pushed on the data stack. Actually, the constants defined by CONSTANT and the variables defined by VARIABLE are still verbs in Forth language. They instruct the Forth computer to introduce new data items to the data stack. However, their usage is equivalent to that of numbers, and they are best described as 'pseudo-nouns'.

Semantically, a constant is equivalent to its preassigned number, and a variable is equivalent to an address in the RAM memory, as shown in Table 3.

VOCABULARY creates subgroups of instructions in the dictionary as vocabularies. When the name of a vocabulary is invoked, the vocabulary is made the context vocabulary which is searched first by the interpreter. Normally the dictionary in a Forth computer is a linearly linked list of instructions. VOCABULARY creates branches to this trunk dictionary so that the user can specify partial searches in the dictionary. Each branch is characterized by the end of the linked list as a link address. To execute an instruction defined by VOCABULARY is to store this link address into memory location named CONTEXT. Hereafter, the text interpreter will first search the dictionary starting at this link address in CONTEXT when it receives an instruction from the input stream.

Instructions defined by VOCABULARY are used to switch context in Forth. If all instructions were given unique names, the text interpreter sould be able to locate them uniquely without any ambiguity. The problem arises because the user might want to use the same names for different instructions. This problem is especially acute for single character instructions, which are favored for instructions used very often to reduce the typing chore and to reduce the size of source text. The number of usable ASCII characters limits the choices. The second useful attribute of vocabularies is that instructions of related functionality can be grouped into vocabulary modules using vocabulary instructions. Context can then be switched conveniently from one vocabulary to another. Instructions with identical names can be used unambiguously if they are placed in different vocabularies.

1.8. CREATE DEFINING INSTRUCTIONS

Forth is an interpretive language with a multitude of interpreters. This is the reason why Forth can afford to have very simple syntax structure. An instruction is known to a user only by its name. The user needs no information on which interpreter will actually execute the instruction. The interpreter which interprets the instruction is specified by the instruction itself, in its code field which points to an executable routine. This executable routine is executed at run-time and it interprets the information contained in the body of the instruction. Instructions created by one defining instruction share the same interpreter. The interpreter which executes code instructions is generally called the inner interpreter. The interpreter which interprets high level colon instructions is called the address interpreter, because a colon instruction is equivalent to a list of addresses. Constants and variables also have their respective interpreters.

A defining instruction must perform two different tasks when it is used to define a new user instruction. To create a new instruction, the defining instruction must compile the new instruction into the dictionary, constructing the name field, link field, code field which point to the appropriate interpreter, and the parameter field which contains pertinent data making up the body of this new instruction. The defining instruction must also contain an interpreter which will execute the new instruction at runtime. The address of this interpreter is inserted into the code field of all user instructions created by this defining instruction. The defining instruction is a combination of a compiler and an interpreter in conventional programming terminology. A defining instruction constructs new user instructions during compilation and executes the instructions it created at run-time. Because a user instruction uses the code field to point to its interpreter, no explicit syntax rule is necessary for different types of instructions. Each instruction can be called directly by its name. The user does not have to supply any more information except the names, separated by delimiters.

The most exciting feature of Forth as a programming language is that it not only provides many resident defining instructions as compiler- interpreters, but also supplies the mechanism for the user to define new defining instructions to generate new classes of instructions or new data structures tailored to specific applications. This unique feature in Forth amounts to the capability of extending the language by constructing new compilers and new interpreters. Normal programming activity in Forth is to build new instructions, which is similar to writing program and program modules in conventional languages. The capability to define new defining instructions is extensibility at a high level in the Forth language. This unique feature cannot be found in any other programming languages.

There are two methods to define a new defining instruction as shown in Table 4. The :-<BUILDS-DOES>-; construct creates a defining instruction with an interpreter defined by high level instructions very similar to a structure list in a regular colon definition. The interpreter structure list is put between DOES> and ';'. The compilation procedure is contained between <BUILDS and DOES>. Since the interpreter will be used to execute all the instructions created by this defining instruction, the interpreter is preferably coded in machine codes to increase execution speed. This is accomplished by the :-<BUILDS-;CODE- construct. The compilation procedure is specified by instructions between <BUILDS and ;CODE. Data following ;CODE are compiled as machine codes which will be used as an interpreter when the new instruction defined by this defining instruction is executed at run-time.

TABLE 4. CREATING NEW DEFINING INSTRUCTIONS

```
<high-level defining instruction> ::=

CREATE<delimiter><compiler structure ist>{DOES>}
<delimiter> <interpreter structure list>;

( : <high-level defining instruction> CREATE
<structure list> DOES> <structure list> ; )


<low-level defining instruction> ::=
    CREATE<delimiter><compiler structure list>;
    CODE<delimiter> <interpreter assembly code list>


( : <low-level defining instruction> CREATE <structure
    list> ;CODE <interpreter assembly code list> )


<compiler structure list> ::=
    <structure list>

<interpreter structure list> ::=
    <structure list>

<interpreter assembly code list> ::=
    <assembly code list>
```

1.9. CONCLUSION

Computer programming is a form of art, far from being a discipline of science or engineering. For a specified programming problem, there are essentially an infinite number of solutions, entirely depending upon the programmer as an artisan. However, we can rate a solution by its correctness, its memory requirement, and its execution speed. A solution by default must be correct. The best solution has to be the shortest and the fastest. The only way to achieve this goal is to use a computer with an instruction set optimized for the problem. Optimization of the computer hardware is clearly impractical because of the excessive hardware and software costs. Thus, one would have to compromise by using a fixed, general purpose instruction set offered by a real computer and its language compiler. To solve a problem with a fixed instruction set, one has to write programs to circumvent the shortcomings of the instruction set.

The solution in Forth is not arrived at by writing programs, but by creating a new instruction set in the Forth virtual computer. The new instruction set in essence becomes the solution to the programming problem. This new instruction set can be optimized at various levels for memory space and for execution speed, including hardware optimization. Forth allows us to surpass the fundamental limitation of an computer, which is the limited and fixed instruction set. This limitation is also shared by conventional programming languages, though at a higher and more abstract level.

Forth as a programming language allows programmers to be more creative and productive, because it enables them to mold a virtual computer with an instruction set best suited for the problems at hand. In this sense, Forth is a revolutionary development in the computer science and technology.

CHAPTER 2. The FigForth MODEL

2.1. Forth as an Operating System

A real computer is rather unfriendly. It can only accept instructions in the form of ones and zeros. The instructions must be arranged correctly in proper sequence in the core memory. Registers in the CPU must be properly initialized. The program counter must then be set to point to the beginning of a program in memory. After the start signal is given to the computer, it runs through the program at a lightening speed, and ends often in a unredeemable crash. An operating system is a program which changes the personality of a computer and makes it more friendly to the user. After the operating system is loaded into the core memory and is initialized, the computer is transformed into a virtual computer, which responds to high level commands similar to natural English language and performs specific functions according to the commands. After it completes a set of commands, it will come back and politely ask the user for a new set of commands. If the user is slow in responding, it will wait patiently.

An operating system also manages all the resources in a computer system for the user. Hardware resources in a computer are the CPU time, the core memory, the I/O devices, and disk memory. The software resources include editor, assembler, high level language compilers, program library, application programs and also data files. It is the principal interface between a computer and its user, and it enables the user to solve his problem intelligently and efficiently.

Conventional operating systems in most commercial computers share two common characteristics: monstrosity and complexity. A typical operating system on a minicomputer occupies a volume in the order of megabytes and it requires a sizable disk drive for normal functioning. A small root program is memory resident. This root program allows a user to call in a specified program to perform a specific task. Each program called uses a peculiar language and syntax structure. To solve a typical programming problem, a user must learn about six to ten different languages under a single operating system, such as a Command Line Interpreter, an Editor, an Assembler or a Macro-assembler, one or more high level languages compilers, a Linker, a Loader, a Debugger, a Librarian, a File Manager, etc. The user is entirely at the mercy of the computer vendor as far as the systems software is concerned.

FigForth is a complete operating system in a very small package. A figForth system, including a text interpreter, a compiler, an editor, and an assembler, usually requires only about 8K bytes. The whole system is memory resident and all functions are available for immediate execution. It provides a friendly programming environment to solve many programming problems. The same language and syntax rules are used in all phases of program development.

The bulk of this operating system is in the dictionary, which contains all the executable procedures, instructions, and some system parameters necessary for the whole system to operate. After the dictionary is loaded into the computer memory, the computer is transformed into a virtual Forth computer. In this virtual Forth computer, the memory is divided into many areas to hold different information. A memory map of a typical fig-Forth operating system is shown in Fig. 1, which requires about 16K bytes of memory.

2.2. MEMORY MAP

At the bottom of the memory are the dictionary and boot-up literals. They comprise the basic Forth system to be loaded into memory when the system is initialized upon power-up. The dictionary grows toward higher memory when new definitions are compiled. Immediately above the dictionary is a word buffer. When a text string is fed into the text interpreter, it is first parsed out and then moved to this area to be interpreted or to be compiled.

About 68 bytes above the dictionary are reserved for the word buffer. Above the word buffer is the output text buffer which temporarily holds texts to be output to a terminal or other devices. The starting address of the output text buffer is contained in a user variable PAD . This text buffer is of indefinite size as it grows toward high memory. It should be noted that the text buffer moves upward as the dictionary grows because PAD is offset from the top of dictionary by 68 bytes. The information put into the text buffer must be used before new definitions are compiled.

The next area is a free memory space which can be used by the dictionary from below or by the data stack from above. The data stack grows downward from high memory to low memory as data are pushed on it. Data stack contracts back to high memory as data are popped off. If too many definitions are compiled to the dictionary and too many data items are pushed on the data stack, the data stack might clash against the dictionary, because the free space between them is physically limited. At this point, it is better to clean up the dictionary. If the dictionary cannot be reduced, more memory space should be allocated between the data stack and the dictionary, involving the reconfiguration of the system.

Above the data stack is an area shared by the terminal input buffer and the return stack. The terminal input buffer is used to store a line of text the user typed on the console terminal. The whole line is moved into the terminal input buffer for the text interpreter to process. The terminal input buffer grows toward high memory and the return stack grows from the other end toward low memory. Usually 256 bytes are reserved for return stack and terminal input buffer. This space is sufficient for normal operation. The return stack clashes into the input buffer only when the return stack is handled improperly which would in any case cause the system to crash.

Above the return stack is the user area where many system variables called user variables are kept. These user variables control the system configurations which can be modified by the user to dynamically reconfigure the system at run-time. The functions of these user variables will be discussed later in this Chapter.

The last memory area on the top of the memory is the disk buffers. The disk buffers are used to access the mass storage as the virtual memory of the Forth system. Data stored on disk are read in blocks into these buffers where the Forth system can use them much the same as data stored in regular memory. The data in disk buffers can be modified. Modified data or even completely new data written into the buffers can be put back to disk for permanent storage. The sizes and the number of disk buffers depend upon the particular installation and the characteristics of the disk drive.

2.3. INSTRUCTION SET

The virtual fig-Forth computer recognizes a rather large set of instructions, and it can execute these instructions interactively. The instructions most often used in programming are summarized in Tables 5 to 9. They are grouped under the titles of stack instructions, input/output instructions, memory and dictionary instructions, defining instructions and control structures, and miscellaneous instructions.

This instruction set covers a very wide spectrum of activities. At the very lowest level, primitive instructions manipulate bits and bytes of data on the data stack and in the memory. These primitive instructions are coded in the machine codes of the host computer, and they are the ones that turn a real computer into a Forth virtual computer. At a higher level, instructions can perform complicated tasks, such as text interpretation, accessing virtual memory, creating new instructions, etc. All high level instructions ultimately refer to the primitive instructions for execution. This very rich instruction set allows a user to solve many programming problems conveniently and to optimize the solutions for performance.

TABLE 5. STACK INSTRUCTIONS

Operand Keys: n 16-bit integer, u 16-bit unsigned integer, d 32-bit signed double integer, addr 16-bit address, b 8-bit byte, c 7-bit ASCII character, and f boolean flag.

DUP (n - n n)   Duplicate top of stack.

DROP (n -)   Discard top of stack.

SWAP (n1 n2 - n2 n1)   Reverse top two stack items.

OVER (n1 n2 - n1 n2 n1)   Copy second item to top.

ROT (n1 n2 n3 - n2 n3 n1)   Rotate third item to top.

-DUP (n - n ?)   Duplicate only if non-zero.

>R (n -)   Move top item to return stack.

R> (- n)	Retrieve item from return stack.	
R (- n)	Copy top of return stack onto stack.	
+ (n1 n2 - sum)	Add.	
D+ (d1 d2 - sum)	Add double-precision numbers.	
- (n1 n2 - diff)	Subtract (n1-n2).	
* (n1 n2 - prod)	Multiply.	
/ (n1 n2 - quot)	Divide (n1/n2).	
MOD (n1 n2 - rem)	Modulo (remainder from division).	
/MOD (n1 n2 - rem quot)	Divide, giving remainder and quotient.	
*/MOD (n1 n2 - rem quot)	Multiply, then divide (n1*n2/n3), with double-precision intermediate.	
*/ (n1 n2 - quot)	Like */MOD, but give quotient only.	
MAX (n1 n2 - max)	Maximum.	
MIN (n1 n2 - min)	Minimum.	
ABS (n - absolute)	Absolute value.	
DABS (d - absolute)	Absolute value of double-precision number.	
MINUS (n - -n)	Change sign.	
DMINUS (d - -d)	Change sign of double-precision number.	
AND (n1 n2 - and)	Logical bitwise AND.	
OR (n1 n2 - or)	Logical bitwise OR.	
XOR (n1 n2 - xor)	Logical bitwise exclusive OR.	
< (n1 n2 - f)	True if n1 less than n2.	
> (n1 n2 - f)	True if n1 greater than n2.	
= (n1 n2 - f)	True if n1 equal to n2.	

0< (n - f)	True if top number negative.
0= (n - f)	True if top number zero.

TABLE 6. INPUT-OUTPUT INSTRUCTIONS

. (n -)	Print number.
.R (n u -)	Print number, right-justified in u column.
D. (d -)	Print double-precision number.
D.R (d u -)	Print double-precision number in u column.
CR (-)	Do a carriage-return.
SPACE (-)	Type one space.
SPACES (u -)	Type u spaces.
." (-)	Print message (terminated by ").
DUMP (addr u -)	Dump u numbers starting at address.
TYPE (addr u -)	Type u characters starting at address.
COUNT (addr - addr+1 u)	Change length byte string to TYPE form.
?TERMINAL (- f)	True if terminal break request present.
KEY (- c)	Read key, put ASCII value on stack.
EMIT (c -)	Type ASCII character from stack.
EXPECT (addr u -)	Read u characters (or until carriage-return) from input device to address.
WORD (c -)	Read one word from input stream, delimited by c.
NUMBER (addr - d)	Convert string at address to double number.
<# (-)	Start output string.

# (d1 - d2)	Convert one digit of double number and add character to output string.
#S (d - 0 0)	Convert all significant digits of double number to output string.
SIGN (n d - d)	Insert sign of n to output string.
#> (d - addr u)	Terminate output string for TYPE.
HOLD (c -)	Insert ASCII character into output string.
DECIMAL (-)	Set decimal base.
HEX (-)	Set hexadecimal base.
OCTAL (-)	Set octal base.

TABLE 7. MEMORY AND DICTIONARY INSTRUCTIONS

@ (addr - n)	Replace word address by contents.
! (n addr -)	Store second word at address on top.
C@ (addr - b)	Fetch one byte only.
C! (b addr -)	Store one byte only.
? (addr -)	Print contents of address.
+! (n addr -)	Add second number to contents of address.
CMOVE (from to u -)	Move u bytes in memory.
FILL (addr u b -)	Fill u bytes in memory with b beginning at address.
ERASE (addr u -)	Fill u bytes in memory with zeros.
BLANKS (addr u -)	Fill u bytes in memory with blanks.
HERE (- addr)	Return address above dictionary.
PAD (- addr)	Return address of scratch area.

ALLOT (u -)	Leave a gap of n bytes in the dictionary.
, (n -)	Compile number n into the dictionary.
' (- addr)	Find address of next string in dictionary.
FORGET (-)	Delete all definitions above and including the following definition.
DEFINITIONS (-)	Set current vocabulary to context vocabulary.
VOCABULARY (-)	Create new vocabulary.
FORTH (-)	Set context vocabulary to Forth vocabulary.
EDITOR (-)	Set context vocabulary to Editor vocabulary.
ASSEMBLER (-)	Set context vocabulary to Assembler.
VLIST (-)	Print names in context vocabulary.

TABLE 8. DEFINING INSTRUCTIONS AND CONTROL STRUCTURES

: (-)	Begin a colon definition.
; (-)	End of a colon definition.
VARIABLE (n -) (- addr)	Create a variable with initial value n. Return address when executed.
CONSTANT (n -) (- n)	Create a constant with value n. Return the value n when executed.
CODE (-)	Create assembly-language definition.
;CODE (-)	Create a runtime code routine in assembly codes.
<BUILDS...DOES>	Create a new defining word, with runtime code routine in high-level Forth.

DO   (end+1 start -)   Set up loop, given
                                    index range.

LOOP   (-)   Increment index, terminate loop if equal
                                    to limit.

+LOOP   (n -)   Increment index by n. Terminate loop
                                    if outside limit.

I   (- index)   Place loop index on stack.

LEAVE   (-)   Terminate loop at next LOOP or +LOOP.

IF   (f -)   If top of stack is true, execute true clause.

ELSE   (-)   Beginning of the false clause.

ENDIF   (-)   End of the IF-ELSE structure.

BEGIN   (-)   Start an indefinite loop.

UNTIL   (f -)   Loop back to BEGIN until f is true.

REPEAT   (-)   Loop back to BEGIN unconditionally.

WHILE   (f -)   Exit loop immediately if f is false.

TABLE 9. MISCELLANEOUS INSTRUCTIONS

((-)   Begin comment, terminated by).

ABORT   (-)   Error termination of execution.

SP@   (- addr)   Return address of top stack item.

LIST   (screen -)   List a disk screen.

LOAD   (screen -)   Load a disk screen (compile or execute).

BLOCK   (block - addr)   Read disk block to memory address.

UPDATE   (-)   Mark last buffer accessed as updated.

FLUSH   (-)   Write all updated buffers to disk.

EMPTY-BUFFERS   (-)   Erase all buffers.

2.4. SYSTEM CONSTANTS AND USER VARIABLES

Some system constants defined in figForth are listed in Table 10. User variables are listed in Table 11. Most of the user variables are pointers pointing to various areas in the memory map to facilitate memory access.

TABLE 10. SYSTEM CONSTANTS

FIRST   3BE0H. Address of the first byte of the disk buffers.

LIMIT   4000H. Address of the last byte of disk buffers plus one, pointing to the free memory not used by the Forth system.

B/SCR   8 Blocks per screen. In the fig-Forth model, a block is 128 bytes, the capacity of a disk sector. A screen is 1024 bytes used in editor.

B/BUF   128. Bytes per buffer.

C/L   64. Characters per line of input text.

BL   32. ASCII blank.

TABLE 11. USER VARIABLES

S0   Initial value of the data stack pointer.

R0   Initial value of the return stack pointer.

TIB   Address of the terminal input buffer.

WARNING   Error message control number. If 1, disk is present, and screen 4 of drive 0 is the base location of error messages. If 0, no disk is present and error messages will be presented by number. If -1, execute (ABORT) on error.

FENCE   Address below which FORGETting is trapped.
To forget below this point the user must alter the contents
of FENCE .

DP   The dictionary pointer which contains the next free memory
above the dictionary. The value may be read by HERE and
altered by ALLOT .

VOC-LINK   Address of a field in the definition of the most recently
created vocabulary. All vocabulary names are linked by
these fields to allow control for FORGETing through
multiple vocabularies.

BLK   Current block number under interpretation. If 0, input is
being taken from the terminal input buffer.

IN   Byte offset within the current input text buffer (terminal or
disk) from which the next text will be accepted.
WORD uses and moves the value of IN .

OUT   Offset in the text output buffer. Its value is incremented
by EMIT. The user may alter and examine OUT to control
output display formatting.

SCR   Screen number most recently referenced by LIST .

OFFSET   Block offset to disk drives. Contents of OFFSET is added
to the stack number by BLOCK .

CONTEXT   Pointer to the vocabulary within which
dictionary search will first begin.

CURRENT   Pointer to the vocabulary in which new
definitions are to be added.

STATE   If 0, the system is in interpretive or
executing state. If non-zero, the system is in
compiling state. The value itself is
implementation dependent.

BASE   Current number base used for input and
output numeric conversions.

DPL	Number of digits to the right of the decimal point on double integer input. It may also be used to hold output column location of a decimal point in user generated formatting. The default value on single number input is - 1.
FLD	Field width for formatted number output.
CSP	Temporarily stored data stack pointer for compilation error checking.
R#	Location of editor cursor in a text screen.
HLD	Address of the latest character of text during numeric output conversion.

2.5. SIMPLE COLON DEFINITIONS

In the figForth model, many arithmetic and logical instructions are Forth high level definitions or colon definitions. They serve very well as some simple examples in programming and extending the basic Forth word set. Some of them are listed here with their definitions:

: -   MINUS + ;

: =   - 0= ;

: <   - 0< ;

: >   SWAP < ;

: ROT   >R SWAP R> SWAP ;

: -DUP   DUP IF DUP ENDIF ;

Many memory operations which affect large areas of memory are also defined at a high level as colon definitions. FILL is a basic word used to define many others. The definition of FILL is presented here in the vertical format, which will be used extensively in our future discussions.

: FILL   addr n b --

Fill n bytes of memory beginning at addr with the same value of byte b.

SWAP >R	store n on the return stack
OVER C!	store b in addr
DUP 1+	addr+1, to be filled with b
R> 1-	n-1, number of bytes to be filled by CMOVE
CMOVE	A primitive. Copy (addr) to (addr+1), (addr+1) to (addr+2), etc , until all n locations are filled with b.

;

FILL is used to define ERASE which fills a memory area with zero's, and BLANKS which fills with blanks (ASCII 32).

: ERASE   **0 FILL ;**

: BLANKS   **BL FILL ;**   BL=32, a defined constant

CHAPTER 3. TEXT INTERPRETER

The text interpreter, or the outer interpreter, is the operating system in a Forth computer. It is absolutely essential, that the reader understand it completely before proceeding to other sections. Many of the properties of Forth language, such as compactness, execution efficiency and ease in programming and utilization, are embedded in the text interpreter. When the Forth computer is booted up, it immediately enters into the text interpreter. In the default interpretive state, the Forth computer waits for the operator to type a line of commands on his console terminal. The command text string he types on the terminal, after a carriage return being entered, is then parsed by the text interpreter and appropriate actions will be performed accordingly.

To make the discussion of text interpreter complete, we shall start with the definition, COLD , meaning starting the computer from cold. COLD calls ABORT . ABORT calls QUIT where the text interpreter, properly named INTERPRET , is embedded. These definitions are discussed in this sequence. It is rather strange to start the text interpreter with words like ABORT and QUIT . The reason will become apparent when we discuss the error handling procedures. After an error is detected, the error handling procedure will issue an appropriate error message and call ABORT or QUIT depending upon the seriousness of the error.

This major Forth monitoring loop is schematically shown in Fig. 2. Although nothing new is shown in the flow chart, it is hoped that a graphic diagram will make a lasting impression on the reader to help him understand more clearly the concepts discussed here.

: COLD   --

The cold start procedure. Adjust the dictionary pointer to the minimum standard and restart via ABORT . May be called from terminal to remove application program and restart.

EMPTY-BUFFERS	Clear all disk buffers by writing zero's from FIRST to LIMIT.
0 DENSITY !	Specify single density diskette drives.
FIRST USE !	Store the first buffer address in USE and PREV , preparing for disk accessing.
FIRST PREV !	
DR0	Select drive 0 by setting OFFSET to 0.
0 EPRINT !	Turn off the printer.
ORIG	Starting address of Forth codes, where initial user variables are kept.
12H +	
UP @ 6 +	User area
10H CMOVE	Move 16 bytes of initial values over to the user area. Initialize the terminal.
ORIG 0CH + @	Fetch the name field address of the last word defined in the trunk Forth vocabulary, and
FORTH 6 + !	Store it in the FORTH vocabulary link. Dictionary searches will start at the top of FORTH vocabulary. New words will be added to FORTH vocabulary unless another vocabulary is named.
ABORT	Call ABORT , the warm start procedure.
;	

CHAPTER 4. THE ADDRESS INTERPRETER

The function of the text or outer interpreter is to parse the text from the input stream, to search the dictionary for the word parsed out, and to handle numeric conversions if dictionary searches failed. When a matching entry is found, the text interpreter compiles its code field address into the dictionary, if it is in a state of compilation. However, if it is in state of execution and the entry is of the immediate type, the text interpreter just leaves the code field address on the data stack and calls on the address interpreter to do the real work. The address interpreter works on the machine level in the host computer, hence it is often referred to as the inner interpreter.

If a word to be executed is a high level Forth definition or a colon definition, which has a list of code field addresses in its parameter field, the address interpreter will properly interpret these addresses and execute them in sequence. Hence the name address interpreter. The address interpreter uses the return stack to dig through many levels of nested colon definitions until it finds a code definition in the Forth nucleus. This code definition consisting of machine codes is then executed by the CPU. At the end of the code definition, a jump to NEXT instruction is executed, where NEXT is a run-time procedure returning control to the address interpreter, which will execute the next definition in the list of execution addresses. This process goes on and on until every word involved in every nesting level is executed. Finally, the control is returned back to the text interpreter.

The return stack allows colon definitions to be nested indefinitely, and to correctly unnest them after the primitive code definitions are executed. The address interpreter with an independent return stack thus very significantly contributes to the hierarchical structure in the Forth language which spans from the lowest machine codes to the highest possible construct with a uniform and consistent syntax.

To diskuss the mechanisms involved in the address interpreter, it is necessary to touch upon the host CPU and its instruction set on which the Forth virtual computer is constructed. Here I have chosen to use the PDP-11 instruction set as the vehicle. The PDP-11 is a stack oriented CPU, sharing many characteristics with the Forth virtual machine. All the registers have predecrementing and postincrementing facilities very convenient to implement the stacks in Forth. The assembly codes using the PDP-11 instructions thus allow the very concise and precise definition of functions performed by the address interpreter.

The Forth virtual machine uses four PDP-11 registers for stacks and address interpretation. These registers are named as follows:

SP   **Data stack pointer**

RP   **Return stack pointer**

IP   **Interpretive pointer**

W   **Current word pointer**

The data stack pointer and the return stack pointer point to the top of their respective stacks. The familiar stack operators like DUP, OVER, DROP, etc and arithmetic operators modify the contents as well as the number of items on the data stack. However, the user normally does not have access to the interpretive pointer IP nor the word pointer W . IP and W are tools used by the address interpreter.

The word NEXT is a run-time routine of the address interpreter. IP usually points to the next word to be executed in a colon definition. After the current word is executed, the contents of IP is moved into W and now IP is incremented, pointing to the next word to be executed. Now, W contains the address of the current word to be executed, and an indirect jump to the address in W starts the execution process of this word. In the mean time, W is also incremented to point to the parameter field address of the word being executed. All code definitions ends with the routine NEXT, which allows the next word after this code definition to be pulled in and executed.

In PDP-11 figForth, NEXT is defined as a macro rather than an independent routine. This macro is expanded at the end of all code definitions.

NEXT:

MOV (IP)+,W	Move the content of IP, which points to the next wordto be executed, into W . Increment IP , pointing to the second word in execution sequence.
JMP @(W)+	Jump indirect to code field address of the next word. Increment W so it points to the parameter field of this word. After the jump, the run-time routine pointed to by the code field of this word will be executed.

If the first word in the called word is also a colon definition, one more level of nesting will be entered. If the next word is a code definition, its code field contains the address of its parameter field, i.e., the code field address plus 2. Here, JMP @(W)+ will execute the codes in the parameter field as machine instructions. Thus, the code field in a word determines how this word is to be interpreted by the address interpreter.

To initiate the address interpreter, a word EXECUTE takes the address on the data stack, which contains the code field address of the word to be executed, and jump indirectly to the routine pointed to by the code field.

CODE EXECUTE   cfa --

Execute the definition whose code field address cfa is on the datastack.

MOV (S)+,W	Pop the code field address into W , the word pointer
JMP @(W)+	Jump indirectly to the code routine. Increment W to point to the parameter field.

In most colon definitions, the code field contains the address of a run-time routine called DOCOL, meaning 'DO the COLon routine', which is the 'address interpreter' for colon definitions.

DOCOL: Run-time routine for all colon definitions.

MOV IP,-(RP)   Push the address of the next word to the return stack and enter a lower nesting level.

MOV W,IP   Move the parameter field address into IP , pointing to the first word in this definition.

MOV (IP)+,W

JMP @(W)+   These two instructions are the macro NEXT . The old IP was saved on return stack and the new IP is pointing to the word to be executed. NEXT will bring about the proper actions .

Using the interpretive pointer IP alone would only allow the processing of a address list at a single level. The return stack is used as an extension of IP. When a colon definition calls other colon definitions, the contents of IP are saved on the return stack so that the IP can be used to call other definitions in the called colon definition. DOCOL thus provides the mechanism to nest indefinitely within colon definitions.

At the end of a colon definition, execution must be returned to the calling definition. The analogy of NEXT in colon definitions is a word named ;S, which does the unnesting.

CODE ;S   --

Return execution to the calling definition. Unnest one level.

MOV (RP)+,IP   Pop the return stack into IP , pointing now to the next word to be executed in the calling definition.

NEXT   Go ahead executed the word pointed to by IP . We shall not repeat the definition of NEXT which is MOV (IP)+,W JMP @(W)+ .

The interplay among the four registers, IP , W , RP , and S allows the colon definitions to nest and to unnest correctly to an indefinite depth, limited only by the size of the return stack allocated in the system. This process of nesting and unnesting is a major contributor to the compactness of the Forth language. The overhead of a subroutine call in Forth is only two bytes, identifying the address of the called subroutine.

A few variations of NEXT are often defined in figForth for many microprocessors as endings of code definitions. PDP-11 figForth did not use them because of the versatility of the PDP-11 instruction set. Nevertheless, these endings are presented here in PDP codes for completeness and consistency.

PUSH: --

Push the contents of the accumulator to the data stack and return to NEXT .

MOV 0,-(S)   Push 0 register to data stack

NEXT

POP: --

TST (S)+   Diskard the top item of data stack

NEXT   Return

PUT: --

Replace the top of data stack with the contents of the accumulator, here register 0, and NEXT return.

MOV 0,(S)

NEXT

LIT: --

Push the next word to the data stack as a literal. Increment IP and skip this literal. NEXT Return. LIT is used to compile numbers into the dictionary. At run-time, LIT pushes/ the in-line literal to the data stack to be used in computations.

MOV (IP)+,-(S)

NEXT

A point of the 'Forth loop'.

CHAPTER V. COMPILER

The Forth computer spends most of its time waiting for the user to type in some commands at the terminal. When it is actually doing something useful, it is doing one of two things: executing or interpreting words with the address interpreter, or parsing and compiling the input texts from the terminal or disk. These are the two 'states' of the Forth computer when it is executing. Internally, the Forth system uses an user variable STATE to remind itself what kind of job it is supposed to be doing. If the contents of STATE is zero, the system is in the executing state, and if the contents of STATE is not zero, it is in the compiling state. Two instructions are provided for the user to switch explicitly between the executing state and the compiling state. They are '[', left-bracket, and ']', right-bracket.

: [--

Suspend compilation and execute the words following [up to]. This allows calculation or compilation exceptions before resuming compilation with]. Used in a colon definition in the form:

: nnnn -- [--] -- ;

0 STATE !   Write 0 into the user variable STATE and switch to executing state.

; IMMEDIATE   [must be executed, not compiled.

:]   --

Resume compilation till the end of a colon definition.

C0H STATE !   The text interpreter compares the value stored in STATE with the value in the length byte of the definition found in the dictionary. If the definition is an immediate word,

its length byte is greater than
C0H because of the precedence and the sign bits
are both set.
Setting STATE to C0H will force non-immediate words
to be compiled and immediate words to be executed,
thus entering into the 'compiling state'.

;

In either state, the text interpreter parses a text string out of the input stream and searches the dictionary for a matching name. If an entry, a word of the same name, is found, its code field address will be pushed to the data stack. Now, if STATE is zero, the address interpreter is called in to execute this word. If STATE is not zero, the text interpreter itself will push this code field address to the top of dictionary, and compile this word into the body of a new definition the text interpreter is working on. Therefore, the text interpreter is also the compiler in the figForth system, and it is very much optimized to do compilation just as efficiently as interpretation.

There are numerous instances when the compiler cannot do its job to build complicated program structures. The compiler itself can only compile linear list of addresses, one word after another. If program structures require branching and looping, as in the BEGIN--UNTIL, IF--ELSE--ENDIF, and DO--LOOP constructs, the compiler needs lots of help from the address interpreter. The help is provided through words of the IMMEDIATE nature, which are immediately executed even when the system is in the compiling state. These immediate words are therefore compiler directives which direct the compiling process so that at run-time the execution sequences may be altered.

In this Chapter, we shall first discuss the words which create a header for a new definition in the dictionary. These are words which start the compiling process. In Chapter 12 we shall discuss the immediate words which construct conditional or unconditional branch to take care of special compilation conditions.

A dictionary entry or a word must have a header which consists of a name field, a link field, and a code field. The body of the word is contained in the parameter field right after the code field. The header is created by the word CREATE and its derivatives, which are called defining words because they are used to create or define different classes of words. All words in the same class have the same code field address in the code fields. The code field address points to a code routine which will interpret this word when this word is to be executed. The structure of a definition as compiled in the dictionary is shown in Fig. 4.

: CREATE   --

Create a dictionary header for a new definition with name cccc . The new word is linked to the CURRENT vocabulary. The code field points to the parameter field, ready to compile a code definition. Used in the form:

CREATE cccc

BL WORD	Bring the next string delimited by blanks to the top of dictionary.
HERE	Save dictionary pointer as name field address to be linked.
DUP C@	Get the length byte of the string
WIDTH @ WIDTH	has the maximum number of characters allowed in the name field.
MIN	Use the smaller of the two, and
1+ ALLOT	allocate space for name field, and advance DP to the link field.
DUP 0A0H TOGGLE	Toggle the eighth (start) and the sixth (smudge) bits in the length byte of the name field. Make a 'smudged' head so that dictionary search will not find this name .
HERE 1- 80H TOGGLE	Toggle the eighth bit in the last character of the name as a delimiter to the name field.
LATEST ,	Compile the name field address of the last word in the link field, extending the linking chain.

CURRENT @ !   Update contents of LATEST in the current
                                vocabulary.

HERE 2+ ,   Compile the parameter field address into
                                code field, for the convenience of a new
                                code definition. For other types of definitions,
                                proper code routine address will be
                                compiled here.

;

: CODE   --

Create a dictionary header for a code definition. The code field contains its
parameter field address. Assembly codes are to be compiled (assembled)
into the parameter field.

CREATE   Create the header, nothing more to be done on the header.

[COMPILE]

ASSEMBLER   Select ASSEMBLER vocabulary as the CONTEXT vocabulary,
                which has all the assembly mnemonics and words pertaining
                to assembly processes.

;

CHAPTER 6. ERROR HANDLING

The figForth model provides very extensive error checking procedures to ensure compiler security, so that compilation results in correct and executable definitions. To facilitate error checking and reporting, fig-Forth model maintains a user variable WARNING and one or more disk blocks containing error messages.

The user variable WARNING controls the actions taken after an error is detected. If WARNING contains 1, a disk is present and screen number 4 in Drive 0 is supposed to be the base location of all error messages. If WARNING contains 0, no disk is available and error messages will be reported simply by an error number. If WARNING contains -1, the word (ABORT) will be executed. The user can modify the word (ABORT) to define his own error checking policy. In the fig-Forth model, (ABORT) calls ABORT which restarts the system (warm start). The error handling process is best shown in a flow chart in Fig. 5.

: ?ERROR   f n --

Issue error message n if the boolean flag f is true.

SWAP   Test the flag f.

IF ERROR   True. Call ERROR to issue error message.

ELSE DROP   No error. Drop n and return to caller.

ENDIF

;

: ERROR   n -- in blk

Issue error message and restart the system. FigForth saves the contents in IN and BLK on stack to assist in determining the location of error.

WARNING @ 0<	See if WARNING is -1,
IF (ABORT)	if so, abort and restart.
ENDIF	
HERE COUNT TYPE	Print name of the offending word on top of the dictionary.
." ?"	Add a question mark to the terminal.
MESSAGE	Type the error message stored on disk.
SP!	Clean the data stack.
IN @	
BLK @	Fetch IN and BLK on stack for the operator to look at if he wishes.
QUIT	Restart the Forth loop.
;	

: (ABORT)   --

Execute ABORT after an error when WARNING is -1. It may be changed to a user defined procedure.

ABORT ;

CHAPTER VII

TERMINAL INPUT AND OUTPUT

The basic primitives handling terminal input and output in FORTH are KEY and EMIT . The definitions of than depend on the host ocmputer and its hardware configurations. It is sufficient to mention here that KEY accepts a keystroke from the terminal keyboard and leaves the ASCII code of the character of this key on the data stack. EMIT pops an ASCII character from the data stack and transnits it to the terminal for display. EMIT also increments the variable OUT for any character it puts out.

The ward that causes a line of text to be reai in frcm the terminal is EXPECT. A flow chart shows graphirally how EXPECT processes characters typed in through the terminal.

: EXPECT	addr n —
	Transfer n characters frcm the terminal to menory starting at addr. The text may be terminated by a carriage return. An ASCII NUL is appended to the end of text.
OVER +	address, the end of text.
OVER	Start Of text
DO	Repeat the following for n times
KEY	Get one character from terminal
DUP	Make a copy
0EH +ORIGIN	Get the ASCII code of input buzk-space
=	

IF	If the input is a back-space
DROP	Discard the back-space still on stack.
8	Replace it with the back-space for the output device
OVER	Copy addr
I =	See if the current charcter is the first chararter of text
DUP	Copy it,to be used as a flag.
R> 2 - +	Get the loop index. Decrement it by 1 if it is the starting character, or decrement it by 2 if it is in the middle of the text.
>R	Put the corrected loop index back on return stack.
-	If the back-space is the first character, ring the bell. Otherwise, output back-spade and decrement character count.
ELSE	Not a back-space
DUP 0DH =	Is it a carriage-return?
IF	Yes, it is carriage return
LEAVE	Prepare to exit the loop. CR is end of text line.
DROP BL	Drop CR iron the stack and replace with a blank.
0	Put a null on stack.
ELSE DUP	Input is a regular ASCII character. Make a copy.
ENDIF	
I C!	Store the ASCII chararter into the input buffer area.
0 I 1+ !	Guard the text with an ASCII NUL.
ENDIF	End of the input loop

EMIT	Echo the input charazter to terminal
LOOP	Loop back if not the en? of text.
DROP	Discard the addr remaining on stack.
;	

: QUERY	Input B0 characters (or until a carriage-return) from the terminal and place the text in the terminal input buffer.
TIB	TIB contains the starting address of the input terminal buffer.
50H EXPECT	Get 80 charmters.
0 IN !	Set the input character counter IN to 0. Text parsing shall begin at TIB .

The work horse in the text interpreter is the word WORD , which parses a string delimited by a specified ASCII charcter frcm the input buffer and places the string into the word buffer on top of the dictionary.

The string in the word buffer is in the correct form for a name field in a new definition. It may be processed otherwise as required by the text interpreter. A flow diagram of WORD is show in Fig. 7, followed by a more detailed description.

: WORD	c -------
	Read text from the input stream until a delimiter c is encountered. Store the text string at the top of dictionary starting at HERE . The first byte is the character count, then the text string, and two or more blanks. If BLK is zero, input it from the terminal; otherwise, input from the disc block referred to by BLK .
BLK @	BLK=0?
IF	BLK is not zero, go lodr at the disc.
BLK @	The BLOCK number

BLOCK Grab a block of data frcm disc and pit it in a disc buffer. Leave the buffer address on the stack. BLOCK is the word to access disc virtual menory.

ELSE BLK=0, input is from terminal

TIB @ Text should be put in the terminal input buffer.

ENDIF

IN @ IN contains the character offset into the current input text buffer.

+ Add offset to the starting adaiess of buffer, pointing to the next character to be read in.

SWAP Get delimiter c over the string addras.

ENCLOSE A primitive word to scan the text. From the byte address and the delimiter c , it determines the byte offset to the first non-delimiter character, the offset to the first delimiter after the text string, and the offset to the next character after the delimiter. If the string is delimited by a NUL , the last offst is equal to the previous offset.
(addr c — addr nl n2 n3)

HERE 22H BLANKS write 34 blanks to the top of dictionary.

IN +! Increment IN by the character count, pointing to the next text string to be parsed.

OVER - >R Save n2-n1 on return stack.

R HERE C! Store character count as the length byte at HERE .

+ Buffer addrss + nl, starting point of the text string in the text buffer.

HERE 1+ Adiress after the length byte on dictionary.

R> Get the chararter count back from the return stack.

;   Move the string from input buffer to top of dictionary.

The text string moved over to the top of the dictionary is in the correct form for a new header, should a new definition be created. It is also in the right form to be compared with other entries in the dictionary for a matching name. After the text string is placed at HERE , the text intertreter will be able to process it.

Following are words fcr typing string data to the output terminal.

:TYPE   addr n -—

         Transmit n chararters frcm a text string stored at addr
         to the terminal.

-DUP   Copy n if it is not zero.

IF   n is non-zero

   OVER +   addr+ n , the end of text

   SWAP   addr, start of text

   DO   Loop to type n characters

    I C@   Fetch character frcm text

   EMIT   Typeout

   LOOP

   ELSE   n =0, no output

   DROP   Discard addr

   ENDIF

;

Since lots of text strings processed by the text interpreter have a character count as the first byte of the string, sud: as the name field of a word, a special word COUNT is defined to prepare this type of strings to be typed out by TYPE.

: COUNT   addr1 --- addr2 n
                      Push the address and byte count n of a text string at add:-1
                      to the data stack. The first byte of the text string is a
                      byte oount. COUNT is usually followed by TYPE .

  DUP 1+   addr2=addr1+1

  SWAP   Swap addrl over addr2 and fetch the byte count to the stack .

If the text string contains lots of blanks at the erxi, there is no use to type them out. A utility word -TRAILING can he used to strip off these trailing blanks so that scme I/0 time can be saved. The ocmmand to type out a long text string is

addr COUNT -TRAILING TYPE

: -TRAILING   addr n1 ---- addr n2
                      Adjust the character count n1 of a text string at addr
                      to suppress trailing blanks.

DUP 0

DO   Scan n1 chararters

OVER OVER   Copy addr and nl

+ 1 -   addr+n1-1, the address of the last chararter in the string.

C@ BL -   See if it is a blank

IF LEAVE   Not a blank. Exit the loop.

ELSE 1-   Blank. n2-=n1-1 is now on the stack.

ENDIF

LOOP   Loop back, decrementing nl until a non-blank character
                      is found, terminating the loop.

;

In a colon definition, sometimes it is necessary to include message to be typed out at runtime to alert the operator, or to indicate to him the progress of the program. These messages can be coded inside a definition using the command

." text string --—   "

The word **."** will cause the text string up to **"** to be typed out. The definition of **."** uses a runtine procedure **(.")** which will be discussed first.

: (.")	Rumtime procedure compiled by ." to type an in—line text string to the terminal.
R	Copy IP from the return stack, which points to the beginning of the in-line text string.
COUNT	Get the length byte of the string, preparing for TYPE .
DUP 1+	Length + 1
R> + >R	Increment IP on the return stack by 1ength+1, thus skip the text string and point to the next word after " , which is the next wcrd to be executed.
TYPE	Now type out the text string.
;	
: ."	Compile an in-line text delimited by the trailing " . Use the procedure (.") to type this text to the terminal.
22H	ASCII value of the delimiter " .
STATE @	Compiling or executing?
IF	Compiling state
COMPILE (.")	Compile the code field address of (.) so it will type out text at rumtime.
WORD	Fetch the text string delimited by " , and store it on top of dictionary, in-line with the compiled adresses.

HERE C@	Fetch the length of string
1+ ALLOT	Have the dictionary pointer parsing the text string. Ready to compile the next word in the same definition.
ELSE	Executing state
WORD	Get the text to HERE , on top of dictionary.
HERE	Start of text string, ready to be typed out.
ENDIF	
;	

IMMEDIATE	This word ." must be executed immediately in the Compiling state to process the text string after it. IMMEDIATE toggle the precedence bit in the name field of ." to make an 'immediate word' .
: ID.	nfa ----- Print an entry's name from its name field address on stack.
PAD	Output text buffer address
20H	ASCII blank
5FH FILL	Fill PAD with as 95 blanks
DUP PFA LFA	Find the link field address
OVER -	lfa-nfe, character count
PAD SWAP CMOVE	Move the entire name with the length wte to PAD
PAD COUNT	Prepare string for output
01FH AND	No more than 31 characters
TYPE	Type out the name
SPACE	Append a space.
;	

It is necessary to move the name to PAD for output, because the length byte in the name field contains extra bits which contain important information not to be disturbed by output procedures.

The basic word to print out text storage on disc is .LINE , which prints out a line (64 characters} of text in a screen. .LINE is also used to output error messages stored on disc, and to display screens of texts in the editor.

: .LINE   line scr ---
Print on the terminal a line of text frcn disc by its line number and screen number scr given on stack. Trailing blanks are also supressed.

(LINE)   Runtime procedure to convert the line number and the screen number to disc buffer address containing the text.

-TRAILING TYPE   Type out the text.

;

:(LINE)   line scr -—- addr count

>R   Save scr on return stack.

C/L B/BUF */MOD   Calculate the character offset and the screen offset members from the line number, characters/line, and bytes/buffer.

R> B/SCR * +   Calculate the block number frcm scr , blocks/scr, and the buffer number left by */MOD.

BLOCK   Call BLOCK to get data from disc to the disc buffer, and leave the buffer address on stack.

+	Add character offset to buffer address to get the starting address of the text.
C/L	64 characters/line
;	

: LIST	n —
	Display the ASCII text of screen n on the terminal.
DECIMAL CR	Switch to decimal base ard output a carriage-return.
DUP SCR !	Store n into SCR to be used by the editor.
." SCR # " .	Print the screen nunber n first.
10H 0 DO	Print the text in 16 lines of 64 characters each.
CR I 3 .R SPACE	Print line nunber.
I SCR @ .LINE	Call .LINE to print one line of text.
LOOP CR ;	Output a carriage return after the 1611': line.

CHAPTER 8. NUMERIC CONVERSIONS

A very important task of the text interpreter is to convert numbers from a
human readable form into a machine readable form and vice versa. Forth
allows its user the luxury of using any number base, be it decimal, octal,
hexadecimal, binary, radix 36, radix 50, etc. He can also switch from one
base to another without much effort. The secret lies in a user variable
named BASE which holds the base value used to convert a machine binary
number for output, and to convert a user input number to binary. The
default value stored in BASE is decimal 10. It can be changed by

: HEX   10H   BASE ! ;   to hexadecimal,

: OCTAL   8H   BASE ! ;   to octal, and

: DECIMAL 0AH BASE ! ;   back to decimal.

The simple command n BASE ! can store any reasonable number into BASE to
effect numeric conversions.

The word NUMBER is the workhorse converting ASCII represented numbers
to binary and pushing the result on the data stack. The word sequence <# #S
#> converts a number on top of the stack to its ASCII equivalent for output to
terminal. These words and their close relatives are discussed in this Chapter.
The overall view on the process of converting a string to its binary numeric
representation is shown in Fig. 8.

: (NUMBER)   d1 addr1 --- d2 addr2

Run-time routine of number conversion.   Convert an ASCII text beginning at
addr1+1 according to BASE. The result is accumulated with d1 to become
d2. addr2 is the address of the first unconvertable digit.

BEGIN

    1+ DUP >R   Save addr1+1, address of the first digit, on return stack.

    C@   Get a digit

BASE @	Get the current base
DIGIT	A primitive. (c n1 -- n2 tf or ff) Convert the character c according to base n1 to a binary number n2 with a true flag on top of stack. If the digit is an invalid character, only a false flag is left on stack.
WHILE	Successful conversion, accumulate into d1.
SWAP	Get the high order part of d1 to the top.
BASE @ U*	Multiply by base value
DROP	Drop the high order part of the product
ROT	Move the low order part of d1 to top of stack
BASE @ U*	Multiply by base value
D+	Accumulate result into d1
DPL @ 1+	See if DPL is other than -1
IF	DPL is not -1, a decimal point was encountered
1 DPL +!	Increment DPL, one more digit to right of decimal point
ENDIF	
R>	Pop addr1+1 back to convert the next digit.
REPEAT	If an invalid digit was found, exit the loop here. Otherwise repeat the conversion until the string is exhausted.
R>	Pop return stack which contains the address of the first non-convertable digit, addr2.
;	

: NUMBER   addr -- d

Convert character string at addr with a preceding byte count to signed double integer number, using the current base. If a decimal point is encountered in the text, its position will be given in DPL. If numeric conversion is not possible, issue an error message.

0 0 ROT — Push two zero's on stack as the initial value of d .

DUP 1+ C@ — Get the first digit

2DH = — Is it a - sign?

DUP >R — Save the flag on return stack.

+ — If the first digit is -, the flag is 1, and addr+1 points to the second digit. If the first digit is not -, the flag is 0. addr+0 remains the same, pointing to the first digit.

-1 — The initial value of DPL

BEGIN — Start the conversion process

DPL ! — Store the decimal point counter

(NUMBER) — Convert one digit after another until an invalid char occurs. Result is accumulated into d .

DUP C@ — Fetch the invalid digit

BL - — Is it a blank?

WHILE — Not a blank, see if it is a decimal point

DUP C@ — Get the digit again

2EH - — Is it a decimal point?

0 ?ERROR — Not a decimal point. It is an illegal character for a number. Issue an error message and quit.

0 — A decimal point was found. Set DPL to 0 the next time.

REPEAT — Exit here if a blank was detected. Otherwise repeat the conversion process.

DROP — Discard addr on stack

R>   Pop the flag of - sign back

IF DMINUS   Negate d if the first digit is a - sign.

ENDIF

;   All done. A double integer is on stack.

: <#   --

Initialize conversion process by setting HLD to PAD.   The conversion is done on a double integer, and produces a text string at PAD.

PAD   PAD is the scratch pad address for text output, 68 bytes
                above the dictionary head HERE .

HLD !   HLD is a user variable holding the address of the last
                character in the output text string.

;

CHAPTER 9. DICTIONARY

In a Forth computer, the dictionary is a linked list of named entries or words which are executed when called by name. The dictionary consists of procedures defined either in assembly codes (code definitions) or in high level codes (colon definitions). It also contains system information as constants and variables used by the system. Inside the computer, the dictionary is maintained as a stack, growing from low memory towards high memory as new definitions are compiled or assembled into the dictionary. When the text interpreter parses out a text string form the input stream, the text is moved to the top of dictionary. If the text is the name of a new definition, it will be left there for the compiling process to continue. If it is not a new definition, the text interpreter will try to find a word in the dictionary with a name matching the string. The word found in the dictionary will be executed or compiled depending on the state of the text interpreter. The dictionary is thus the bulk of a Forth system, containing all the necessary information necessary to make the whole system work.

The dictionary as a stack is maintained by a user variable named DP, the dictionary pointer, which points to the first empty memory location above the dictionary. A few utility words move DP around to effect various functions involving the dictionary.

: HERE   -- addr

DP @   Fetch the address of the next available memory location
                    above the dictionary.

;

: ALLOT   n --

DP +!   Increment dictionary pointer DP by n, reserving n bytes
                    of dictionary memory for whatever purposes intended.

;

: ,   n --

Store n into the next available cell above dictionary and advance DP by 2, i. e., compile n into the dictionary.

HERE !   Store n into dictionary

2 ALLOT   Point DP above n, the number just compiled.

;

In fact, ',' (comma) is the most primitive kind of a compiler. With it alone, theoretically we can build the complete dictionary, or compile anything and everything into the dictionary. All the compiler words and assembler words are simple or complicated derivatives of ','. This feature is clearly reflected in the nomenclature of assembly mnemonics in the Forth assembler in which all mnemonics end with a comma.

For byte oriented processors, C, is defined to compile a byte value into the dictionary:

: C,   b --

Enter a byte b on dictionary and increment DP by 1.

HERE C!

1 ALLOT

;

: -FIND   -- pfa b tf , or ff

Accept the next word delimited by blanks in the input stream to HERE, and search the CONTEXT and then the CURRENT vocabularies for a matching name. If found, the entry's parameter field address, a length byte, and a true flag are left on stack. Otherwise only a boolean false flag is left.

BL WORD   Move text string delimited by blanks from input string
                  to the top of dictionary HERE .

HERE   The address of text to be matched.

CONTEXT @ @ Fetch the name field address of the last word defined in the CONTEXT vocabulary and begin the dictionary search.

(FIND)   A primitive. Search the dictionary starting at the address on stack for a name matching the text at the address second on stack. Return the parameter field address of the matching name, its length byte, and a boolean true flag on stack for a match. If no match is possible, only a boolean false flag is left on stack.

DUP 0=   Look at the flag on stack

IF   No match in CONTEXT vocabulary

  DROP   Discard the false flag

  HERE   Get the address of text again

  LATEST   The name field address of the last word defined in the CURRENT vocabulary

  (FIND)   Search again through the CURRENT vocabulary.

ENDIF

;

Please note the order of the two dictionary searches in -FIND .The first search is through the CONTEXT vocabulary. Only after no matching word is found there, is the CURRENT vocabulary then searched. This searching policy allows words of the same name to be defined in different vocabularies. Which word gets executed or compiled by the text interpreter will depend upon the 'context' in which the word was defined. A sophisticated Forth system usually has three vocabularies: the trunk FORTH vocabulary which contains all the system words, an EDITOR vocabulary which allows a programmer to edit his source codes in screens, an an ASSEMBLER vocabulary which has all the appropriate assembly mnemonics and control structure words. The user can create his own vocabulary and put all his applications words in it to avoid conflicts with words defined in the system.

A good example is the definition of the trunk vocabulary of all the Forth system words:

VOCABULARY FORTH IMMEDIATE

All vocabularies have to be declared IMMEDIATE, so that context can be switched during compilation. After FORTH is defined as above, whenever FORTH is encountered by the text interpreter, the interpreter will set the user variable CONTEXT to point to the second cell of the parameter field in the FORTH definition, which maintains the name field address of the last word defined in the FORTH vocabulary as the starting word to be searched. Using the phrase

FORTH DEFINITIONS

will set both the CONTEXT and the CURRENT to point to FORTH vocabulary so that new definitions will be added to the FORTH vocabulary. The words VOCABULARY and DEFINITIONS are defined as:

: VOCABULARY   --

A defining word used in the form

  VOCABULARY cccc

to create a new vocabulary with name cccc . Invoking cccc will make it the context vocabulary which will be searched by the text interpreter.

<BUILDS	Create a dictionary entry with following text string as its name, and the code field pointing to the word after DOES> .
0A081H ,	A dummy header at vocabulary intersection.
CURRENT @	Fetch the parameter field address pointing to the last word defined in the current vocabulary.

CFA ,   Store its code field address in the second cell in
       parameter field.

HERE   Address of vocabulary link.

VOC-LINK @ , Fetch the user variable VOC-LINK and insert it in the
       dictionary.

VOC-LINK ! Update VOC-LINK with the link in this vocabulary.

DOES>   This is the end in defining cccc vocabulary. The next words
       are to be executed when the name cccc is invoked.

2 + CONTEXT ! When cccc is invoked, the second cell in its parameter field
       will be stored into the variable CONTEXT . The next
       dictionary search will begin with the cccc vocabulary.

;

: DEFINITIONS --

Used in the form: cccc DEFINITIONS Make cccc vocabulary the current
vocabulary. Hence new definitions will be added to the cccc vocabulary.

CONTEXT @

CURRENT !

;

The header of a dictionary entry is composed of a name field, a link field, and
a code field. The parameter field coming after the header is the body of the
entry. The name field is of variable length from 2 to 32 bytes, depending on
the length of the name from 1 to 31 characters in the figForth model. The
first byte in the name field is the length byte. The first and the last bytes in
the name field have their most significant bits set as delimiting indicators.
Therefore, knowing the address of any of the fields in the header, one can
calculate the addresses of all other fields. Different field addresses are used
for different purposes. The name field address is used to print out the name,

the link field address is used in dictionary searches, the code field address is used by the address interpreter, and the parameter field address is used to access data stored in the parameter field. To facilitate the conversions between the addresses, a few words are defined as follows:

: TRAVERSE   addr1 n -- addr2

Move across the name field of a variable length name field. addr1 is the address of either the length byte or the last character. If n=1, the motion is towards high memory; if n=-1, the motion is towards low memory. addr2 is the address of the other end of the name field.

SWAP	Get addr1 to top of stack.
BEGIN	
OVER +	Copy n and add to addr, pointing to the next character.
7FH	Test number for the eighth bit of a character
OVER C@	Fetch the character
<	If it is greater than 127, the end is reached.
UNTIL	Loop back if not the end.
SWAP DROP	Discard n.
;	

: LFA   pfa -- lfa

Convert the parameter field address to link field address.

4 - ;

: CFA   pfa -- cfa

2 - ;

Convert the parameter field address to code field address.

: NFA   pfa -- nfa

Convert the parameter field address to name field address.

5 -   The end of name field

-1 TRAVERSE   Move to the beginning of the name field.

;

: PFA   nfa -- pfa

Convert the name field address to parameter field address.

1 TRAVERSE   Move to the end of name field.

5 +   Parameter field.

;

: LATEST   -- addr

Leave the name field address of the last word defined in the current vocabulary.

CURRENT @ @ ;

To locate a word in the dictionary, a special word ' (tick) is defined to be used in the form:

           ' cccc

to search for the name cccc in the dictionary.

: '   -- pfa

Leave the parameter field address of a dictionary entry with a name cccc. Used in a colon definition as a compiler directive, it compiles the parameter field address of the word into dictionary as a literal. Issue an error message if no matching name is found.

-FIND Get cccc and search the dictionary, first the context and then current vocabularies.

0= 0 ?ERROR Not found. Issue error message.

DROP Matched. Drop the length byte.

[COMPILE] Compile the next immediate word LITERAL to compile the parameter field address at run-time.

LITERAL

;

IMMEDIATE must be immediate to be useful in a colon definition.

All the previous discussions are on words which add or compile data to the dictionary. In program development, one will come to a point that he has to clear the dictionary of some words no longer needed. The word FORGET allows him to discard some part of the dictionary to reclaim the dictionary space for other uses.

: FORGET --

Used in the form:

FORGET cccc

Delete definitions defined after and including the word cccc. The current and context vocabulary must be the same.

CURRENT @ CONTEXT

@ - 18 ?ERROR Compare current with context, if not the same, issue an error

[COMPILE] ' Locate cccc in the dictionary.

DUP Copy the parameter field address

FENCE @ Compare with the contents in the user variable FENCE ,

< 15 ?ERROR If cccc is less than FENCE , do not forget. FENCE guards the trunk FORTH vocabulary from being accidentally forgotten.

DUP NFA Fetch the name field address of cccc, and

DP ! store in the dictionary pointer DP . Now the top of dictionary is redefined to be the first byte of cccc , in effect deleting all definitions above cccc .

LFA @ Get the link field address of cccc pointing to the word just below it.

CURRENT @ ! Store it in the current vocabulary, adjusting the current vocabulary to the fact that all definitions above (including) cccc no longer exist.

;

A powerful word VLIST prints of the names of all entries defined in the context vocabulary to allow the programmer to peek at the definitions in the dictionary.

: VLIST --

List the names of all entries in the context vocabulary. The 'break' key on terminal will terminate the listing.

80H OUT ! Initialize the output character counter OUT to print 128 characters.

CONTEXT @ @ Fetch the name field address of the last word in the context vocabulary.

BEGIN

    OUT @   Get the output character count

    C/L >   If it is larger than characters/line of the output device,

    IF

      CR 0 OUT ! output a CR/LF and reset OUT .

    ENDIF

    DUP ID.   Type out the name and

    SPACE SPACE   add two spaces.

PFA LFA @   Get the link pointing to previous word.

    DUP 0=   See if it is zero, the end of the link,

    ?TERMINAL OR   or if the break key on terminal was pressed.

UNTIL   Exit at the end of link or after break key was pressed; otherwise continue the listing of names.

DROP   Discard the parameter field address on stack and return.

;

CHAPTER 10. VIRTUAL MEMORY

In a computer system, the core memory or the semiconductor memory is a limited and the most expensive resource which users wished to be infinite. Since it is physically impossible to have infinite amount of memory inside a computer, the next best thing is the magnetic disk memory using hard disks or floppy diskettes. Because the characteristics of the disk memory is very much different from those of the core memory, the use of disk memory often requires some device handlers to transfer data or programs between the computer and the disk. In most mainframe computers, disks and other peripherals are treated as files managed by the operating system, which insulates the users from the devices. The usage of the disk memory in high level language thus needs a fair amount of software overhead in terms of memory space and execution speed.

Forth treats the disk as a direct extension of the core memory in blocks of B/BUF bytes. A user can read from these blocks and write to them much the same as he is reading or writing the core memory. Thus the disk memory becomes a virtual memory of the computer. The user can use it freely without the burdens of addressing the disk and managing the I/O. Implementing this virtual memory concept in the Forth system makes available the entire disk to the user, giving him essentially unlimited memory space to solve his problem.

Disk memory in Forth is organized into blocks of B/BUF bytes. The blocks are numbered sequentially from 0 to the disk capacity. Forth system maintains an area in high memory as disk buffers. Data from the disk are read into the buffers, and the data in buffers can be written back to disk. As implemented in the figForth model, each disk buffer is 132 bytes long, corresponding to 128 byte/sector in disk with 4 bytes of buffer information. The length of buffer can be changed by modifying the constant B/BUF which is the number of bytes the disk spits out each time it is accessed, usually one sector. B/BUF must be a power of 2 (64, 128, 256, 512, or 1024). The constant B/SCR contains the value of the number of blocks per screen which is used in editing texts from disk. B/SCR is equal to 1024 divided by B/BUF. Disk buffers in memory are schematically shown in Fig. 9, assuming, that each buffer is 132 bytes long.

Several other user variables are used to maintain the disk buffers. FIRST and LIMIT define the lower and upper bounds of the buffer area. LIMIT - FIRST must be multiples of B/BUF + 4 bytes. The variable PREV points to the address of the buffer which was most recently referenced, and the variable USE points to the least referenced buffer, which will be used to receive a new sector of data from disk if requested.

The most important and the most used word to transfer data into and out of the disk is BLOCK. BLOCK calls another word BUFFER to look for an available buffer. BUFFER in turn calls a primitive word R/W to do the actual work of reading or writing the disk. These and other related words are to be discussed here. A flow chart of BLOCK is shown in Fig. 10 for better comprehension.

CHAPTER 11. DEFINING WORDS

The Forth language is a major synthesis of many concepts and techniques used for sometime in the computer industry, such as stacks, dictionary, virtual memory, and the interpreter. The single most important invention by Charles Moore in developing this language which wrapped all these elements tegether and rolled them into a small yet powerful operating system is the code field in the header of a definition. The code field contains the address of a routine to be executed when the definition is called. This routine determines the characteristics of the definition, and interprets the data stored in the parameter field accordingly. In the basic Forth system, only a very small set of code field routines are defined and are used to create many types of definitions often used in programming. The types of definitions commonly used are colon definitions, code definitions, constants, and variables.

The most interesting feature in the Forth language is that the machinery used to define these definitions is accessible to the user for him to create new types of definitions. The mechanism is simply to define new code field routines which will correctly interpret a new class of words. The freedom to create new types of definitions, or in a mind bogging phrase--to define defining words-- was coined as the extensibility of Forth language. The process of adding a new definition to the dictionary--create a header, select the address of a code routine and put in the code field, and compile data or addresses into the parameter field--is termed 'to define a word'. The words like ':', CODE , CONSTANT , VARIABLE , etc., which cause a new word to be defined or compiled into the dictionary, are thus called defining words. The process of generating a word of this kind, the defining word, is 'to define a defining word'. Our subject in this Chapter is how to define a word which defines a class of words.

To create a definition, two things must be done properly: one is to specify how this definition is to be compiled and how this definition is to be constructed in the dictionary; and the second is to specify how this definition is to be executed when it is called by the text interpreter. Consequently, a defining word consists of two parts: one to be used by the compiler to generate a definition in dictionary, and the other part to be executed when the definition is called. All words generated by this defining word will have their code fields containing the same address pointing to the same run-time routine.

There are two ways to define new defining words. If the run-time routine pointed to by the code field is to be defined in machine assembly codes, the format is:

: cccc ---;CODE assembly mnemonics

If the run-time routine is coded in high level words as in a colon definition, the format is:

: cccc <BUILDS --- DOES> --- ;

In the above formats, cccc is the name of the new defining word, --- denotes a series of predefined words, and 'assembly mnemonics' are assembly codes if an assembler has been defined in the dictionary. If there is no assembler in the Forth system, machine codes in numeric form can be compiled into the dictionary to construct the run-time code routine.

Executing the new defining word cccc in the form:

cccc nnnn

will create a new definition nnnn in the dictionary and the words denoted by --- up to ;CODE or DOES> are executed to complete the process of building the definition in the dictionary. The code field of this new definition will contain the address of the routine immediately following ;CODE or DOES> . Consequently, when the newly defined word is called by the interpreter, the run-time routine will be executed.

The above discussion might be somewhat confusing because of the context of defining a defining word. It is. The best way of explaining how the concept works is probably with a lot of examples. Here we shall start with the figForth definitions of ;CODE , <BUILDS , and DOES> , followed by the two simple defining words CONSTANT and VARIABLE . The most useful defining word ':' was discussed previously in Chapter 5 on the compiler. It should be reviewed carefully.

: ;CODE   --

Stop compilation and terminate a new defining word cccc by compiling the run-time routine (;CODE) . Assemble the assembly mnemonics following. Used in the form:

: cccc -- ;CODE assembly mnemonics

?CSP	Check the stack pointer. Issue an error message if not equal to what was saved in CSP by ':' .
COMPILE	When ;CODE is executed at run-time, the address of the next word will be compiled into dictionary.
(;CODE)	Run-time procedure which completes the definition of a new defining word.
[COMPILE]	Compile the next immediate word instead of executing it.
[	Return to executing state to assemble the following assembly mnemonics.
SMUDGE	Toggle the smudge bit in the length byte, and complete the new definition.

;

IMMEDIATE

A class of definitions can then be created by using cccc in the form:

   cccc nnnn

The code fields in nnnn point to the code routine as assembled by the mnemonics following ;CODE in the definition of cccc . The word nnnn when called to be executed will first jump to this code routine and execute this routine at run-time. What will happen afterwards is totally dependent on this code routine. The presence of the code field and hence the execution of the code routine after the word is called makes figForth an indirectly threaded coded system. The code field allows users to extend Forth language to define new data structures and new control structures which are practically impossible in any other high level language. This property is called the extensibility of Forth language.

: (;CODE)   --

The run-time procedure compiled by ;CODE . Rewrite the code field of the most recently defined word to point to the following machine code sequence.

R>   Pop the address of the next instruction off the return stack, which is the starting address of the run-time code routine.

LATEST   Get the name field address of the word under construction.

PFA CFA !   Find the code field address and store in it the address of the code routine to be executed at run-time.

;

The pair of words <BUILDS -- DOES> is used to define new defining words in the form:

          : cccc <BUILDS -- DOES> -- ;

The difference from the ;CODE construct is that <BUILDS-DOES> gives users the convenience of defining the code field routine in terms of other high level definitions, saving them the trouble of coding these routines in assembly mnemonics. Using high level words to define a defining word makes them portable to other types of computers also speaking Forth. The price to be paid is the slower speed in executing words defined by these defining words. This is the tradeoff a user must weigh to his own satisfaction.

: <BUILDS   --

When cccc is executed, <BUILDS will create a new header for a definition with the name taken from the next text in the input stream.

0 CONSTANT   Create a new entry in the dictionary with a zero in its parameter field. It will be replaced by the address of the code field routine after DOES> when DOES> is executed.

;

: DOES>   --

Define run-time routine action within a high level defining word. DOES> alters the code field and the first cell in the parameter field in the defining word, so that when a new word created by this defining word is called, the sequence of words compiled after DOES> will be executed.

R>   Get the address of the first word after DOES> .

LATEST   Get the name field address of the new definition under construction.

PFA !   Store the address of the run-time routine as the first parameter.

;CODE   When DOES> is executed, it will first do the following code routine because ;CODE puts the next address into the code field of CODE> .

DODOE: -- pfa

MOV IP,-(RP)   Push the address of the next instruction on the return stack.

MOV (W)+,IP   Put the address of the run-time routine in IP .

MOV W,-(S)   W was incremented in the last instruction, pointing to the parameter field. Push the first parameter on stack.

NEXT

In the figForth model, there are three often used defining words beside ':' and CODE: CONSTANT, VARIABLE, and USER. They are themselves defined:

: CONSTANT   n --

Create a new word with the next text string as its name and with n inserted into its parameter field.

CREATE	Create a new dictionary header with the next text string.
SMUDGE	Toggle the smudge bit in the length byte in the name field.
,	Compile n into the parameter field.
;CODE	The code field of all constants defined by CONSTANT will have the address of the following code routine:
DOCON:	The constant interpreter.
MOV (W),-(S)	Push the contents of parameter field to the stack.
NEXT	Return to execute the next word.

It is sed in the following form:

n CONSTANT cccc

to define cccc as a new constant. When cccc is later called, the value n will be pushed on the data stack. This is the best way to store a constant in the dictionary for later uses, if this constant is used often. When a number is compiled as an in-line literal in a colon definition, 4 bytes are used because the word LIT must be compile before the literal so that the address interpreter would not mistakenly interpret it as a word address. The overhead of defining a constant is 6 bytes and the bytes needed for name field, averaging to about 10 bytes per definition. If the constant will be used more than thrice, savings in memory space justify the defining of a constant.

: VARIABLE   n --

Define a new word with the following text as its name and its parameter field initialized to n. When the new word is executed, the parameter field address instead of its content is pushed on the stack.

CONSTANT   Create a dictionary header with n in the parameter field. Compiling action in defining a variable is identical to that of defining a constant, but run-time behavior is different.

;CODE   Code field in a variable points to following code routine.

DOVAR: Variable interpreter.

MOV W,-(S)   Push the parameter field address on data stack.

NEXT

Variables are defined by the following commands:

    n VARIABLE cccc

When cccc is later executed, the address of the variable is pushed on the data stack. To get the current value of this variable, one should use the @ command :

    cccc @

and to change the value to a new one n1,

    n1 cccc !

: USER   n --

Create a user variable with n in the parameter field. n is a fixed offset relative to the user area pointer UP for this user variable.

CONSTANT   n is compiled as a constant.

;CODE   The run-time code routine is labelled as DOUSE :

DOUSE: User variable interpreter.

MOV (W),-(S) Push n on data stack.

ADD UP,(S) Add the base address of the user area.

NEXT   Return. Now the top of data stack has the address
          pointing to the user variable.

After a user variable is defined as:

n USER cccc

the word cccc can be called. When cccc is executed, UP+n will be pushed on
the data stack and its contents can be examined by @ or modified by ! . In
figForth, the user variables are used similar to other variables. Their
significance is not apparent because figForth generally does not support
multitasking. When Forth is used in a multitasking environment, each task
owns a copy of all the user variables, which define the context of a task and
allow tasks to be switched conveniently. This is a topic much too advanced
to be discussed here.

CHAPTER 12. CONTROL STRUCTURES

Most definitions in the Forth dictionary are defined by the colon ':' word. They are called colon definitions, Forth definitions, or high level definitions. When the text interpreter sees the word ':', it creates a header using the text string following colon as the name and then enters the compiling state. In the compiling state, the text interpreter reads in a text line from the input stream, parses out strings delimited by blanks, and tries to match them with dictionary entries. If a string matches with a dictionary entry, the code field address of the matching word is added to the parameter field of the new definition under construction. This is what we call the compiling process. The compiling process ends when the terminating word ; or ;CODE is encountered.

When a colon definition is later executed, the word addresses in its parameter field are executed by the address interpreter in the order as compiled. If it is necessary to alter the sequential execution process at run-time, a special word has to be used in the compiling process to set up the mechanism of branching and looping, to build the control structures and the program constructs in the colon definition. These special words are equivalent to compiler directives or assembly directives in conventional computer languages. These words do not become part of the compiled definition, but cause specific actions during compilation to build the control structure into the definition and to ensure its correct execution at run-time. These special words in Forth are characterized by the fact that they all have a precedence bit in the length byte of the name field set to one. Words with precedence bit set are called immediate words because the text interpreter turns these words over to the address interpreter for execution even during compilation.

In this Chapter, we shall concern ourselves with the means by which the following control structures are built in a colon definition:

IF -- ELSE -- ENDIF

BEGIN -- UNTIL

BEGIN -- WHILE -- REPEAT

and

DO -- I -- LEAVE -- LOOP

However, before discussing the detailed definitions of these words, a few utility words should be presented to make the discussions more intelligible. The word COMPILE and [COMPILE] are used to handle special compiling situations. The words BRANCH and 0BRANCH are the actual words which get compiled into the definition to do the branching and looping.

Words in a colon definition are normally compiled into dictionary and their code field address are compiled into the parameter field of the colon definition under compilation. Sometimes the compilation should be delayed to the run-time, i. e., the word is to be compiled not when the colon definition is being compiled, but when the colon definition is later executed. To defer compilation until run-time, the instruction COMPILE must precede the word.

: COMPILE   --

Defer compilation until run-time. When the word containing COMPILE is executed, the code field address of the word following COMPILE is compiled into the dictionary at run-time.

?COMP   Error if not compiling.

R>   Top of return stack is pointing to the next word following COMPILE .

DUP 2+ >R   Increment this pointer by 2 to point to the second word following COMPILE , which will be the next word to be executed. The word immediately following COMPILE should be compiled, not executed.

@ ,   Do the compilation at run-time.

;

Immediate words, because of their precedence bits, are executed during compilation. However, if one wanted to use the word sequence in an immediate word as a regular colon definition, i. e. to compile it in-line, the word [COMPILE] can be used to force the following immediate word to be compiled into a definition. The word [COMPILE] is used in the form

   : xxxx --- [COMPILE] cccc --- ;

in which cccc is the name of an immediate word.

: [COMPILE]   --

Force the compilation of the following immediate word.

-FIND   Accept next text string and search dictionary for a match.

0= 0 ?ERROR   No matching entry was found. Issue an error message.

DROP   Discard the length byte of the found name.

CFA ,   Convert the name field address to code field address and compile it into the dictionary.

;

IMMEDIATE

The two words changing execution sequence in a colon definition are BRANCH and 0BRANCH, both are primitive code definitions. They are of such importance that I feel they should be treated fully. The codes are from PDP-11 fig-Forth.

CODE BRANCH   --

The run-time procedure to branch unconditionally. An in-line offset is added to the interpretive pointer IP to branch forward or backward. BRANCH is compiled by ELSE, AGAIN, and REPEAT.

ADD (IP),IP   Add the contents of the next cell pointed to by IP
to IP itself. The result is put back to IP
which points to the next word to be executed. The
next word can be out of the regular execution order.

NEXT   Return to the word pointed to by IP , completing
the unconditional branching.

CODE 0BRANCH   f --

The run-time procedure to branch conditionally. If f on stack is false (zero),
the following in-line offset is added to IP to branch forward or backward.
Compiled by IF, UNTIL, and WHILE.

TST (S)+   Test the flag f on stack.

BNE ZBRA1   Not zero, continue executing next word by
skipping the offset.

ADD (IP),IP   f is zero, do the branching.

NEXT

ZBRA1:   A common routine shared with LOOP.

ADD #2,IP   f is true, skip the in-line offset. Pick up the
word following the offset and continue execution.

NEXT

Conditional branching in a colon definition uses the forms:

IF (true part) --- ENDIF

or **IF (true part) --- ELSE (false part) --- ENDIF**

At run-time, IF selects to execute the true part of words immediately following it, if the top item on data stack is true (non-zero). If the flag is false (zero), the true part will be skipped to after ELSE to execute the false part. After executing either part, execution resumes after ENDIF . ELSE and the false part are optional. If ELSE part is missing, execution skips to just after ENDIF .

: IF   At run-time   f --
             Compile time   -- addr n

It compiles 0BRANCH and reserves one more cell for an offset value at addr . addr will be used later to resolve the offset value for branching. n is set to 2 for error checking when ELSE or ENDIF is later compiled.

COMPILE 0BRANCH	Compile the code field address of the run-time routine 0BRANCH into the dictionary when IF is executed.
HERE	Push dictionary address on stack to be used by ELSE or ENDIF to calculate branching offset.
0 ,	Compile a dummy zero here, later it is to be replaced by an offset value used by 0BRANCH to compute the next word address.
2	Error checking number.
;	
IMMEDIATE	IF in a colon definition must be executed, not compiled.

: ENDIF   Compile time   addr n --

Compute the forward branching offset from addr to HERE and store it at addr . Test n to match the previous IF or ELSE in the definition.

?COMP   Issue an error message if not compiling.

2 ?PAIRS ENDIF   must be paired with IF or ELSE . If n is
                          not 2, the structure was disturbed
                          or improperly nested.
                          Issue an error message.

HERE   Push the current dictionary address to stack.

OVER -   HERE-addr is the forward branching offset.

SWAP !   Store the offset in addr , thus completing the IF-ENDIF
                      or IF-ELSE-ENDIF construct.

;

IMMEDIATE

: ELSE   Compile time   addr1 n1 -- addr2 n2

Compile BRANCH and reserve a cell for forward branching offset. Resolve the pending forward branching from IF by computing the offset from addr1 to HERE and storing it at addr1 .

2 ?PAIRS   Error checking for proper nesting.

COMPILE BRANCH   Compile BRANCH at run-time when ELSE is executed.

HERE   Push HERE on stack as addr2 .

0 ,   Dummy zero reserving a cell for branching to ENDIF .

SWAP   Move addr1 to top of stack.

[COMPILE] ENDIF   Call ENDIF to work on the offset for forward
branching. ENDIF is an immediate word.
To compile it the word [COMPILE] must be used.

2   Leave n2 on stack for error checking.

;

IMMEDIATE

Indefinite loops are to be constructed using the following forms:

      BEGIN --- UNTIL

or   **BEGIN --- WHILE --- REPEAT**

BEGIN simply leaves the current dictionary address on stack for UNTIL or
REPEAT to pickup and to compute a backward branching offset at the end of
the loop. WHILE is similar to IF in that it skips to just after REPEAT if the flag
on stack at that point isfalse, thus terminating the indefinite loop from inside
the loop. UNTIL terminates the loop only at the end of the loop.

: BEGIN   Compile time   -- addr n

At compile time BEGIN leaves the dictionary address on stack with an error
checking number n. It does not compile anything to the dictionary.

?COMP   Issue an error message if not compiling.

HERE   Push dictionary pointer on stack to be used to compute
backward branching offset.

1   Error checking number.

;

IMMEDIATE

: BACK   addr --

A run-time procedure computing the backward branching offset from HERE
to addr on stack, and compile this offset value in the next in-line cell in the
dictionary.

HERE - ,   addr-HERE, the backward branching offset.

;

: UNTIL   Compile time   addr n --

Compile 0BRANCH and an in-line offset from HERE to addr. Test the error
checking code n. If not equal to 1, there is an error in the nesting structure.

1 ?PAIRS   If n is not 1, issue an error message.

COMPILE 0BRANCH   Compile 0BRANCH at run-time.

BACK   Compute backward branching offset and
                       compile the offset.

;

IMMEDIATE

When the colon definition containing the BEGIN-UNTIL structure is executed,
the word 0BRANCH compiled by UNTIL at the end of a loop will test the flag
on stack at that instant. If the flag is false, 0BRANCH will branch back to the
word following BEGIN. The words between BEGIN and UNTIL will be
repeatedly executed until the flag is true at UNTIL; at this instant, the
interpreter will abort this loop and continue executing the words following
UNTIL.

: AGAIN   compile time   addr n --

Similar to UNTIL but compile BRANCH instead of 0BRANCH in the dictionary to construct an infinite loop. Execution cannot leave this loop unless the words R> DROP are executed in a word inside this loop.

1 ?PAIRS   Error checking.

COMPILE BRANCH   Compile BRANCH and an offset to BEGIN .

BACK

;

IMMEDIATE

The construct BEGIN-WHILE-REPEAT uses WHILE to abort a loop in the middle of the loop. WHILE will test the flag left on stack at that point. If the flag is true, WHILE continues the execution of following words until REPEAT, which then branches unconditionally back to BEGIN. If the flag is false, WHILE causes execution to skip the words up to REPEAT, thus exiting the loop structure.

: WHILE   Compile time   addr1 n1 -- addr1 n1 addr2 n2

Compile 0BRANCH and a dummy offset for REPEAT to resolve. addr1 and n1 as left by BEGIN are also passed on to be processed by REPEAT.

[COMPILE] IF   Call IF to compile 0BRANCH and the offset.

2+   Leave 4 as n2 to be checked by REPEAT .

;

IMMEDIATE

: REPEAT   Compile time   addr1 n1 addr2 n2 --

Compile BRANCH to jump back to BEGIN. Resolve also the branching offset required by WHILE.

>R >R	Get addr2 and n2 out of the way.
[COMPILE] AGAIN	Let AGAIN do the dirty work of compiling unconditional branch back to BEGIN .
R> R>	Restore addr2 and n2 .
[COMPILE] ENDIF	Use ENDIF to resolve the forward branching needed by WHILE .

;

IMMEDIATE

The IF-ELSE-ENDIF and the BEGIN-UNTIL types of constructs simply redirect the execution sequence inside of a colon definition. As discussed previously, the definitions of these compiler directives are quite short and simple, involving only branching and conditional branching. The DO-LOOP type of construct is more complicated because additional mechanisms other than branching are needed to keep track of the loop limits and loop counts. The run-time functions of DO are to take the lower and upper loop limits off the data stack, push them on the return stack, and setup the address for LOOP to jump back. LOOP at run-time will then increment the loop count on top of the return stack and compare its value to that of the loop limit just under it on the return stack. If the loop count equals or exceeds the loop limit, the loop is completed and execution goes to the next word after LOOP. Otherwise, LOOP will branch back to DO and continue the looping. +LOOP behaves similarly to LOOP except that it increments the loop count by a number supplied on the data stack.

The words DO, LOOP, and +LOOP call on their respective run-time routines to do the work. The detailed codes in these run-time routines will be discussed also.

DO-LOOP's are set up in a colon definition in the following forms:

    DO --- I --- LOOP

or   **DO --- I --- +LOOP**

At run-time, DO begins a sequence of repetitive executionscontrolled by a
loop count and a loop limit. The starting value of the loop count and the
loop limit are taken off the data stack at run time. Upon reaching the word
LOOP, the loop count is incremented by one. Until the new loop count
equals or exceeds the loop limit, execution loops back to the word just after
DO. Otherwise, the two loop parameters are removed from the return stack
and the execution continues ahead at the word after LOOP. Within a loop,
the word I will copy the loop count to data stack to be used in computations.

: DO	Run-time	n1 n2 --
	Compile time	-- addr n
COMPILE (DO)	Compile the run-time routine address of (DO) into the dictionary.	
HERE	Address addr for backward branching from LOOP or LOOP. 3 Number for error checking.	
;		
IMMEDIATE		

CODE (DO)	n1 n2 --

The run-time routine starting a DO-LOOP. n1 and n2 are pushed on the
return stack as loop limit and loop index, respectively.

MOV 2(S),-(RP)	Push the loop limit n1 on return stack.
MOV (S),-(RP)	Push the initial loop count n2 on return stack above n1 .
ADD #4,S	Adjust the stack pointer to drop n1 and n2 off the data stack.
NEXT	Return.

CODE I	-- n

Return the current loop index inside a DO-LOOP.

MOV (RP),-(S)   Copy the loop count on return stack and push
it to data stack.

NEXT

CODE LEAVE   --

Make the loop limit equal to the loop count and force the loop to terminate
at LOOP or +LOOP .

MOV (RP),2(RP) Copy loop count to loop limit on the return stack.

 NEXT

 : LOOP   addr n --

Terminate a DO-LOOP structure in a colon definition.

3 ?PAIRS   Check the number left by DO .
                      If it is not 3, issue an error message.
                      The loop is not properly nested.

COMPLIE (LOOP) Compile (LOOP) at run-time when LOOP is executed.

BACK   Compute and compile the backward branch offset.

;

IMMEDIATE

CODE (LOOP)   --

Run-time routine of LOOP .

INC (RP)	Increment the loop count on return stack.
CMP (RP),2(RP)	Compare loop count with the loop limit.
BGE LOOP1	Jump to LOOP1 if the loop count is equal or greater than the loop limit.
ADD (IP),IP	Add backward branch offset to IP and
NEXT	branch back to repeat the DO-LOOP.

LOOP1:

ADD #4,RP	Exit the loop. Discard the loop parameters off the return stack.
ADD #2,IP	Advance IP over the in-line offset number and
NEXT	continue executing the next word after LOOP .

When the loop count must be incremented by an amount other than one, +LOOP should be used to close a DO-LOOP . It is used in the form:

DO --- I --- +LOOP

: +LOOP	Run-time	n1 --
	Compile time	addr n1 --

Increment the loop index by n1 on the stack and test for loop completion. Branch back to DO if not yet done.

3 ?PAIRS	Check n. If it is not 3 as left by DO , issue an error message.
COMPILE (+LOOP)	Compile the address of (+LOOP) at run-time when the colon definition is being built.
BACK	Compile back branch offset.

;

IMMEDIATE

CODE (+LOOP)   n --

Run-time routine at the end of a DO--+LOOP loop.

ADD (S),(RP)   Add n to the loop count on return stack.

TST (S)+   Test and pop data stack

BLT LOOP3   If n is negative, jump to LOOP3 for special processing.

CMP 2(RP),(RP)   n is positive. Compare loop count with loop limit.

BLE LOOP2   If the loop is done, jump to LOOP2 to exit.

ADD (IP),IP   Not yet done, return to DO .

NEXT

LOOP2:

ADD #4,RP   Clear return stack.

ADD #2,IP   Advance IP to the next word after +LOOP .

NEXT

LOOP3:

CMP (RP),2(RP)   Negative increment n . Reverse comparison.

BLE LOOP2

ADD (IP),IP   Not yet done with the loop. Return to the word after DO .

NEXT

CHAPTER 13. EDITOR

In a Forth computer, new definitions are stored in the dictionary in a compiled form. The source text is not saved. Although there are many different ways to recover textual information from the compiled definitions, to 'de-compile' a definition is not the best way to write and edit Forth definitions. As we have discussed in Chapter 10 on the virtual memory, Forth uses the disk to store source text which can be compiled very easily using the word LOAD . To enter source text into the disk memory and to modify them repeatedly during program development and testing, a text editor is indispensable. As in any other language processor, the editor is the principal interface between a programmer and the computer. A good editor makes the programming tasks easier, and in some rare cases enjoyable.

As of now, figForth has yet to have a standardized text editor. In the figForth model, however, there was included a sample text editor by Bill Ragsdale. I will discuss this particular editor in this Chapter. A text editor provides important and extensive examples in using Forth language to handle texts and strings. It is worthwhile for a serious student of the Forth language to go through these examples carefully, to learn techniques in string manipulations.

To facilitate text editing, texts on disk are organized in blocks of 1024 bytes (a unit of screen). Each screen is divided into 16 lines of 64 characters each. A screenful of text thus arranged fits comfortably on the screen of an ordinary CRT terminal, hence the name 'screen'. The text on a screen is most conveniently accessed by lines. A string within a line can be searched and its location indicated by a screen cursor for editing actions, like inserting or deleting characters. A text editor generally performs two quite distinguishable tasks--line editing and string editing. In this figForth sample editor, words are defined separately for these two tasks.

13.1. LINE EDITOR

In the text editor, a screenful of text is maintained in the disk buffers, or the screen buffer. The screen number which denotes the physical location of this screen of text on disk is stored in a user variable SCR. The cursor location in this screen buffer is stored in another user variable R# . Text to be put into the screen buffer or deleted from the screen buffer is temporarily stored in the text buffer area pointed to by the word PAD, which returns the memory address 68 bytes above the dictionary pointer DP. PAD is used as a 'scratch pad' during editing processes, holding text for the screen buffer or strings to be matched with the text in the screen buffer.

Most of the editor definitions have single character names to ease typing during editing. Some of these simple names cause conflects with the names of other definitions defined in the FORTH vocabulary. It is thus advantageous to group all the editing definitions into a separate vocabulary called EDITOR. The EDITOR vocabulary is defined as:

VOCABULARY EDITOR IMMEDIATE

This phrase creates the EDITOR vocabulary which is linked to the trunk FORTH vocabulary. EDITOR when called will make EDITOR the CONTEXT vocabulary, so that definitions defined in EDITOR will be readily accessible in editing screens of text. The phrase

EDITOR DEFINITIONS

makes EDITOR vocabulary also the CURRENT vocabulary. In this way new definitions will be added to the EDITOR vocabulary instead of being treated as regular definitions adding to the FORTH vocabulary.

Two basic utility words are used by the editor to perform the line editing functions. TEXT moves a line of text from the input stream to the text buffer area of PAD. The word LINE computes the line address in the screen buffer. Text lines of 64 characters can then be transferred from PAD to screen buffer or vice versa. We shall first present these two words before getting into the line editing commands.

: TEXT   c --

Move a text string delimited by character c from the dictionary buffer (word buffer) into PAD, blank- filling the remainder of PAD to 64 characters.

HERE	Top of dictionary, beginning of word buffer. The text interpreter puts the text string here.
C/L 1+ BLANKS	Fill word buffer with 65 blanks.
WORD	Move the text, delimited by character c, from the input stream to the word buffer.
PAD	Address of the text buffer.
C/L 1+ CMOVE	Move the text, 64 bytes of text and 1 length byte, to PAD.

;

: LINE   n -- addr

Leave address of the beginning of line n in the screen buffer. The screen number is in SCR. Read the disk block from disk if it is not already in the disk buffers.

DUP FFF0H AND	Make sure n is between 0 and 15.
17 ?ERROR	If not, issue an error message.
SCR @	Get the screen number from SCR .
(LINE)	Read the screen into screen buffer which is composed of the disk buffers. Compute the address of the n'th line in the screen buffer and push it on stack.
DROP	Discard the character count left on stack by (LINE) . Only the line address is left on stack now.

;

: -MOVE   addr n --

Copy a line of text from addr to n'th line in the current screen buffer.

LINE   Get the line address in screen buffer.

C/L CMOVE   Move 64 characters from addr to line n in screen buffer.

UPDATE   Notify the disk handler this buffer has been modified.
                         It will be written back to disk to update the disk storage.

;

: H   n --

Copy n'th line to PAD. Hold the text there ready to be typed out.

LINE   Get the line address.

PAD 1+   Starting address of text in PAD .

C/L DUP PAD C!   Put 64 in the length byte of PAD .

CMOVE   Move one line.

;

: S   n --

Spread n'th line with blanks. Down shift the original n'th and subsequent lines by one line. The last line in the screen is lost.

DUP 1-   Lower limit of lines to be moved.

0EH   14, the last line to be shifted down.

DO

    I LINE   Get thE line address

    I 1+   Next line

    -MOVE   Downshift one line.

1 +LOOP	Decrement loop count and repeat till done.
E	Erase the n'th line.
;	

: D   n --

Delete the n'th line. Move subsequent lines up one line.   The delete line is held in PAD in case it is still needed.

DUP H	Copy the n'th line to PAD.
OFH	The last line.
DUP ROT	Get n to top of stack.
DO	
I 1+ LINE	Next line to be moved.
I -MOVE	Upshift by one line.
LOOP	
E	Erase the last line.
;	

: E   n --

Erase the n'th line in the screen buffer by filling with 64 blanks.

LINE	Line address.
C/L BLANKS	Fill with blanks.
UPDATE	
;	

: R   n --

Replace the n'th line with text stored in PAD.

PAD 1+   Starting address of the text in PAD.

SWAP -MOVE   Move text from PAD to n'th line.

;

: P   n --

Put following text on line n. Write over its contents.

1 TEXT   Accept the following text of C/L characters or till CR to PAD.

R   Put the text into line n.

;

: I   n --

Insert text from PAD to n'th line. Shift the original n'th and subsequent lines down by one line. The last line in the screen is lost.

DUP S   Spread line n and pad with blanks.

R   Move PAD into line n.

;

: CLEAR   n --

Clear the n'th screen by padding with blanks.

SCR !   Store screen number n into SCR .

10H 0 DO   Erase 16 lines

   FORTH I   Get the loop count from return stack. I was redefined by
                    the editor to insert line into a screen. To call the I

which gets the loop count, FORTH must be called to make the trunk FORTH vocabulary the CONTEXT vocabulary, which   is searched first to get the correct I. This demonstrates the use of vocabularies.

EDITOR E   Set the CONTEXT vocabulary back to EDITOR vocabulary to continue editing texts. E will erase the I'th line.

LOOP

;

: COPY   n1 n2 --

Copy screen n1 in drive 0 to screen n2 in drive 1. This is accomplished by reading blocks in screen n1 to disk buffers and changing block numbers to those associated with screen n2. The disk buffers are then flushed back to disk.

B/SCR *   First block in screen n2.

OFFSET @ +   Add block offset for drive 1.

SWAP B/SCR *   First block in screen n1.

B/SCR OVER +   Last block number + 1.

SWAP DO   Go through all blocks in screen n1.

   DUP   Copy block number in screen n2.

   FORTH I   Current block number in screen n1 as the loop count.

   BLOCK   Read the block from screen n1 to disk buffer.

   2 - !   Store the block number in screen n2 into the first cell of the disk buffer, which contains the disk block number. This tricks the system to think the block is in the screen n2.

   1+ T

   UPDATE   Set update bit in disk buffer to be flushed back to disk.

LOOP

DROP   Discard the block number on stack.

FLUSH   Write all disk buffers containing data from screen n1 back
to screen n2, because the block numbers were switched.

;

13.2. STRING EDITOR

The above words belong to what might be called a line editor, which handles
the text by whole lines. The line editor is convenient in inputting lines of
texts. However, if some mistakes are discovered or only a few characters in
a line need to be changed, the line editor is not suitable because one would
have to retype the whole line. Here, a string editor is more effective. The
string editor uses a variable R# as a cursor pointing to a character in a string
which can be accessed by the string editor most easily. The string editor
must be able to search a line or the entire screen for a specified string and
point the cursor to this string. It must have means to delete and modify
characters neighboring the cursor. A colon definition MATCH is used to
search a range of text for a specified string and move the cursor accordingly.
MATCH and a few utility words are used here to build up the word set
involved in the string editor.

: MATCH   addr1 n1 addr2 n2 -- f n3

The text to be searched begins at addr1 and is n1 bytes long. The string to
be matched begins at addr2 and is n2 bytes long. The boolean flag is true if
a match is found. n3 is then the cursor advancement to the end of the
found string. If no match is found, f will be false and n3 be 0.

>R >R 2DUP   Duplicate addr1 and n1.

R> R> 2SWAP Move the copied addr1 and n1 to the top of the stack.

OVER + SWAP Now the stack looks like:
                (addr1 n1 addr2 n2 addr1+n1 addr1 --)

DO	Scan the whole source text.
2DUP	Duplicate addr2 and n2.
FORTH I	The loop index points to source text.
-TEXT	Is the source text here the same as the string at addr2 ?
IF	Yes, the string is found in the text.
>R 2DROP R>	Discard n1 and addr2 on the stack.
- I SWAP -	Offset to the end of the found string.
0 SWAP	Put a boolean underneath.
0 0 LEAVE	Put two dummy zeros on the stack and prepare to leave the loop.
THEN	
LOOP	No match this time. Loop back.
2DROP	Discard garbage on the stack.
SWAP 0= SWAP	Correct the boolean flag upon exit.
;	

: -TEXT	addr1 n addr2 -- f

If the strings at addr1 and addr2 match to n characters, return a true flag. Otherwise, return a false flag.

SWAP -DUP	
IF	If n1 is zero, bypass the tests.
OVER + SWAP	(addr1 addr2+n1 addr2 --)
DO	Scan the string at addr2 .
DUP C@	Fetch a character from the first string.

FORTH I C@   Equal to the corresponding character in
the second string?

IF 0= LEAVE   Not the same. Leave the loop.

ELSE 1+ THEN Continue on.

LOOP

ELSE DROP 0=   n is zero . Leave a false flag. Neither address may be
zero.

THEN

;

The 32-bit double number instructions used in MATCH and -TEXT should be
defined in the FORTH trunk vocabulary as following:

: 2DROP   d --

Discard two numbers from the stack.

DROP DROP ;

: 2DUP   d -- d d

Duplicate a double number.

OVER OVER ;

: 2SWAP   d1 d2 -- d2 d1

Bring the second double number to the top of the stack.

ROT >R   Save top half of the second number.

ROT R>   Move bottom half and restore top half.

;

: TOP   --

Move the cursor to home, top left of the screen.

0 R# !   Store 0 in R# , the cursor pointer.

;

: #LOCATE   -- n1 n2

From the cursor pointer R# compute the line number n2 and the character offset n1 in line number n2.

R# @   Get the cursor location.

C/L /MOD   Divide cursor location by C/L. Line number is the quotient and the offset is the remainder.

;

: #LEAD   -- addr n

From R# compute the line address addr in the screen buffer and the offset from addr to the cursor location n.

#LOCATE   Get offset and line number.

LINE   From line number compute the line address in screen buffer.

SWAP

;

: #LAG   -- addr n

From R# compute the line address addr in the screen buffer and the offset from cursor location to the end of line.

#LEAD	Get the line address and the offset to cursor.
DUP >R	Save the offset.
+	The address of the cursor in screen buffer.
C/L R> -	The offset from cursor to end of line.
;	

: M   n --

Move cursor by n characters. Print the line containing the cursor for editing.

R# +!	Move cursor by updating R#.
CR SPACE	Start a new printing line.
#LEAD TYPE	Type the text preceding the cursor.
5FH EMIT	Print a caret (^) sign at the cursor location.
#LAG TYPE	Print the text after the cursor.
#LOCATE . DROP	Type the line number at the end of text.
;	

: T   n --

Type the n'th line in the current screen. Save the text also in PAD.

DUP C/L *	Character offset of n'th line in the screen.
R# !	Point the cursor to the beginning of n'th line.
H	Move n'th line to PAD.
0 M	Print the n'th line on output device.
;	

: L   --

Re-list the current screen under editing.

SCR @ LIST   List the current screen.

0 M   Print the line containing the cursor.

;

: 1LINE   -- f

Scan a line of text beginning at the cursor location for a string matching with one stored in PAD. Return true flag if a matching string is found with cursor moved to the end of the found string. Return a false flag if no match.

#LAG PAD COUNT   Prepare addresses and character counts to that as required by MATCH .

MATCH   Go matching.

R# +!   Move the cursor to the end of the matching string.

;

: FIND   --

Search the entire screen for a string stored in PAD. If not found, issue an error message. If found, move cursor to the end of the found string.

BEGIN

    3FFH R# @ < Is the cursor location > 1023?

     IF   Yes, outside the screen.

     TOP   Home the cursor.

    PAD HERE C/L 1+ CMOVE   Move the string searched for to HERE to be typed out as part of an error message.

0 ERROR   Issue an error message.

ENDIF

1LINE   Scan one line for a match.

UNTIL

;

: DELETE   n --

Delete n characters in front of the cursor. Move the text from the end of line to fill up the space. Blank fill at the end of line.

>R   Save the character count.

#LAG +   End of line.

FORTH R -   Save blank fill location.

#LAG

R MINUS R# +! Back up cursor by n characters.

#LEAD +   New cursor location.

SWAP MOVE   Move the rest of line forward to fill the deleted string

R> BLANKS   Blank fill to the end.

UPDATE

;

: N   --

Find the next occurrence of the text already in PAD.

FIND   Matching.

0 M   If found, type out the whole line in which the string was found with the cursor properly displayed.

;

: F　　　　　--

Find the first occurrence of the following text string.

1 TEXT　　　Put the following text string into PAD .

N　　　　　Find the string and type out the line.

;

: B　　　　　--

Back the cursor to the beginning of the string just matched.

PAD C@　　　Get the length byte of the text string in PAD .

MINUS M　　Back up the cursor and type out the whole line.

;

: X　　　　　--

Delete the following text from the current line.

1 TEXT　　　Put the text in PAD .

FIND　　　　Go find the string.

PAD C@　　　Get the length byte of the string.

DELETE　　　Delete that many characters.

0 M　　　　Type the modified line.

;

: TILL　　　　--

Delete all characters from cursor location to the end of the following text string.

#LEAD +	The current cursor address.
1 TEXT	Put the following text in PAD .
1LINE	Scan the line for a match.
0= 0 ?ERROR	No match. Issue an error message.
#LEAD + SWAP	The number of characters to be deleted.
DELETE	Delete that many characters and move the rest of line to fill up the space left.
0 M	Type out the new line.
;	

: C   --

Spread the text at cursor to insert the following string. Character pushed off the end of line are lost.

1 TEXT PAD COUNT	Accept text string and move to PAD .
#LAG ROT OVER MIN >R	Save the smaller of the character count in PAD and the number of characters after the cursor.
FORTH R	Get the smaller count
R# +!	Move the cursor by that many bytes
R - >R	Number of characters to be saved.
DUP HERE R CMOVE	Move the old text from cursor on to HERE for temporary storage.
HERE #LEAD + R> CMOVE	Move the same text back. Put at new location to the right, leaving space to insert a string from PAD .

R> CMOVE   Move the new string in place.

UPDATE

 0 M   Show the new line.

;

Are later executed. To defer compilation until run-time, the instruction
COMPILE must precede the word.

: COMPILE

CHAPTER 14. FORTH ASSEMBLERS

An assembler which translates assembly mnemonics into machine codes is equivalent to a compiler in complexity if not more complicated. One might expect the assembler to be simpler because it is at a lower level of construct. However, the large number of mnemonic names with many different modes of addressing make the assembling task much more difficult. In a Forth language system the assembling processes cannot be accomplished by the text interpreter alone. All the resources in the Forth system are needed. For this reason the assembler in Forth is often defined as an independent vocabulary, and the assembling process is controlled by the address interpreter, in the sense that all assembly mnemonics used by the assembler are not just names representing the machine codes but they are actually Forth instructions executed by the address interpreter. These instructions when executed will cause machine codes to be assembled to the dictionary as literals. The data stack and the return stack are often used to assemble proper codes and to resolve branching addresses.

14.1. Three Levels of Forth Assembler

Before discussing codes in the Forth assemblers, I would like to present assemblers in three levels of complexity:

Level 0:   The programmer looks up the machine codes and assembles them to the dictionary;

Level 1:   The computer translates the assembly mnemonics to codes with a lookup-table, but the programmer must fill in addresses and literals when needed; and

Level 2:   The computer does all the work, with mnemonics and operands supplied by the programmer.

The Level 0 Assembler in Forth uses only three definitions already defined in the Forth Compiler:

CREATE   Generate the header for a new code definition,

,   Assemble a 16 bit literal into the dictionary, and

C,   Assemble a byte literal into the dictionary, used in byte oriented processors.

These definitions were described as the most primitive compiler in Chapter 9. They might just as well be the most primitive assembler if the new definition were a code definition. The programmer would write down the machine codes first with the help of those small code cards supplied freely by CPU vendors. The machine codes are entered on the top of the data stack and then assembled to the parameter field of the new definition on top of the dictionary.

The Level 1 Assembler would use the defining word CONSTANT to define assembly mnemonics relating them to their respective machine code. The text interpreter when confronted with a mnemonic name would push the corresponding machine code on the stack. The code will then be assembled to the dictionary by , or C, . An example is:

   0 CONSTANT HALT

which defines HALT as a constant of 0. During assembly, the phrase

      ... HALT , ...

would assemble a HALT instruction into the dictionary. To make it easier for himself, the programmer might want a new definition:

 : HALT,   HALT , ;

Executing HALT, would then assemble the HALT instruction to the dictionary.

Historically all assembler definitions end their names with a comma for the reason just described, indicating that the definition causes a machine instruction to be assembled to the dictionary. This convention serves very well to distinguish assembler definitions from regular Forth definitions.

This scheme in Level 1 Assembler is quite adequate if there were a one to one mapping from mnemonics to machine codes. However, in cases where many codes share the same mnemonic and differ only in operands or addressing mode, the basic code must be augmented to accommodate operands or address fields. It is not difficult to modify definitions as HALT, to make the necessary changes in the code, which has to pass the data stack anyway. To define each assembly mnemonic individually is messy and inelegant. A much more appealing method is to use the <BUILDS-DOES> construct in the Forth language to define whole classes of mnemonics with the same characteristics, which brings us to the Level 2 Assembler.

In the last example of the HALT instruction, instead of using CONSTANT to relate the mnemonic name with the code, a defining word is created as:

: OP   <BUILDS , DOES> @ , ;

The instruction HALT, is then defined by the defining word OP as:

0 OP HALT,   1 OP WAIT,   5 OP RESET, . . .

Now, when HALT, is later processed by the text interpreter, the code 0 is automatically assembled into the dictionary by the runtime routine @ , .

The <BUILDS-DOES> construct can be applied to all other types of assembly mnemonics to assemble different classes of instructions, providing some of the finest examples for the extensibility in the Forth language. No other language can possibly offer such a powerfull tool to its programmers.

A syntactic problem in using the Forth assembler is that before the mnemonics can be executed to assemble a machine code, all the addressing information and operands must be provided on the data stack. Therefore, operands must precede the instruction mnemonics, resulting in the postfix notation. The source listing of a Forth code definition is therefore very different from the conventional assembly source listing, where the operands follow the assembly mnemonic. Using the data stack and the postfix notation greatly facilitate the assembling process in the Forth assembler. This is a very small price to pay for the capability to access the host CPU and to make the fullest use of the resources in a computer system.

Two assemblers will be discussed in this Chapter in an effort to cover the widest range of microprocessors. One is for the homely Intel 8080A which is a byte oriented machine with a rather primitive instruction set. On the other end is the PDP-11 instruction set, which is extensively micro-coded in a 16 bit wide code field. I feel that these two examples should be sufficient to illustrate how Forth assemblers are constructed for most other microprocessors.

14.2.   PDP-11 ASSEMBLER

The PDP-11 instruction set is typical of that for minicomputers. With a 16 bit instruction field, very flexible and versatile addressing schemes are possible comparing with those used in the 8 bit instructions of most common microprocessors. In addition, PDP-11 is a stack oriented machine in which all registers can be used as stack pointers in addition to normal accumulator and addressing functions. There are 8 registers in the PDP-11 CPU: registers 0 to 5 are general purpose registers, register 6 is a dedicated stack pointer, and register 7 is the program counter. Registers can be used in many different addressing modes, making it very convenient to host a Forth virtual machine in the PDP-11 computer. This assembler was programmed by John James and was included in his PDP-11 figForth Model.

The following command sequence must be given first to initiate the ASSEMBLER vocabulary and to prepare the Forth system to build the assembler.

OCTAL   PDP-11 instructions are best presented in octal base
                   because address fields are 6 bits wide.

0 VARIABLE OLDBASE

To ease switching base to and from octal, the currently used base will be stored away in OLDBASE, to be restored when the assembly process is completed.

VOCABULARY ASSEMBLER IMMEDIATE

Create the assembler vocabulary to house all the assembly mnemonics and other necessary definitions.

: ENTERCODE   --

Invoke ASSEMBLER vocabulary to start the assembly process.

[COMPILE] ASSEMBLER	Set CONTEXT to ASSEMBLER to search for the mnemonics.
BASE @ OLDBASE ! OCTAL	Switch base to octal. Save old base to be restored after assembly.
SP@	Push stack pointer on stack for error checking at end.

;

: CODE   --

A more refined defining word to start a code definition.

CREATE	Create a header with the name following CODE .
ENTERCODE	Invoke ASSEMBLER .

;

ASSEMBLER DEFINITIONS

Set both CONTEXT and CURRENT vocabularies to ASSEMBLER . New definitions hereafter will be placed in the assembler vocabulary.

Before discussing the assembler definitions, the PDP-11 CPU registers and their addressing modes should be clarified. An address field uses 6 bits in an instruction. The lower 3 bits specify a register to be referenced for addressing, and the upper 3 bits specify the addressing mode. The register and the addressing mode are combined to form an address field which is used to specify either a source operand or a destination operand in the assembly instruction as required. Registers and modes are defined as follows:

: IS   n --

CONSTANT ;   Short hand for CONSTANT .

0 IS R0   1 IS R1   2 IS R2   3 IS R3   4 IS R4   5 IS R5

6 IS SP   7 IS PC   2 IS W   3 IS U   4 IS IP   5 IS S

6 IS RP

: RTST   r mode -- addr-field -1

Test register r for range between 0 and 7. Add r and mode to form address field addr-field . Also leave a flag -1 on stack to indicate that an address field is underneath.

OVER	Get r to top for tests.
DUP 7 >	Larger than 7 ?
SWAP 0 <	Smaller than 0 ?
OR IF	In either case, issue an error message,
." NOT A REGISTER:"	
OVER . ENDIF	with the offending number appended.
+	addr-field = r + mode
-1	The flag.
;	

The addressing modes are defined as executable definitions using names similar to the operand notation used in PDP assembly language with some twists. The stack effects are:

r -- **addr-field , -1** .

:)+	**20 RTST ;**	Post-increment register mode.
: -)	**40 RTST ;**	Pre-decrement register mode.
: I)	**60 RTST ;**	Indexed register mode.
: @)+	**30 RTST ;**	Deferred post-increment mode.
: @-)	**50 RTST ;**	Deferred pre-decrement mode.
: @I)	**70 RTST ;**	Deferred index mode.

The addressing mode using the program counter is somewhat different from the modes using other general purpose registers.

: #	**27 -1 ;**	Immediate addressing mode.
: @#	**37 -1 ;**	Absolute addressing mode.
: ()	r -- addr-field -1	for register deferred mode.
	n -- n 77 -1	for relative deferred mode.

DUP 10 U<	Top of stack is between 0 and 7, a register.
IF 10 + -1	Make the address field.
ELSE 77 -1 ENDIF	Otherwise, top of stack is an address offset. Make it the relative deferred mode.

;

The simplest instruction requires no operand. These instructions can be defined by a simple defining word:

: OP   n --

A defining word to define instructions without operands.

<BUILDS   Create an header for a mnemonic definition with
                    the mnemonic name following OP .
                    Compile the instruction code on the stack to the
                    parameter field in the new definition.

DOES>   --

                    When the defined mnemonic definition is executed during
                    assembly, execute the following words:

@ ,   Fetch the instruction code stored in parameter field and
                    assemble it to the code definition under construction on
                    top of the dictionary.

;

0 OP HALT,   1 OP WAIT,   2 OP RTI,   3 OP BPT,

4 OP IOT,   5 OP RESET,   6 OP RTT,

241 OP CLC,   242 OP CLV,   244 OP CLZ,   250 OP CLN,

261 OP SEC,   262 OP SEV,   264 OP SEZ,   270 OP SEN,

277 OP SCC,   257 OP CCC,   240 OP NOP,   6400 OP MARK,

Instructions with operands are of course more involved. Those with only one
operand are defined by a defining word 1OP . This word uses many other
utility definitions. However, we shall first present the high level 1OP before
getting into the nitty gritty details of the other low level definitions.

: 1OP   n --

A defining word to define instructions with one operand.

<BUILDS , DOES>   The same defining word format.

@ ,   When the defined word is executed during assembly, the basic instruction code is fetched and assembled to the dictionary.

FIXMODE   Take the mode packet on stack to resolve the address field.

DUP   Copy the address field.

HERE 2 – ORMODE Insert the address field into the lower 6 bit destination field.

,OPERAND   If the instruction needs a 16 bit value either as a literal or as an address, assemble it after the instruction.

;

: FIXMODE   addr-field -1 -- addr-field

                   r -- r

                   n -- n 67

Fix the mode packet on the data stack for ORMODE and ,OPERAND to assemble the instruction correctly.

DUP -1 =   Top of stack = -1 ?

IF DROP   Yes, drop -1 and leave addr-field on top.

ELSE   The top of the stack might be a register or a literal.

   DUP 10 SWAP U<   If top of stack is larger than 7 , PC relative mode.

      IF 67 ENDIF   Push 67 on top of n , indicating PC mode. Otherwise, leave the register number on the stack.

ENDIF

;

: ORMODE   addr-field addr --

Take the address field value addr-field and insert it into the lower 6 bit address field in the instruction code at addr .

SWAP	Move addr-field to top of the stack.
OVER @	Fetch the instruction code at addr .
OR	Insert address field.
SWAP !	Put the modified instruction back.

;

: ,OPERAND   (n) addr-field --

Assemble a literal to the dictionary to complete a program counter addressing instruction.

DUP 67 =	PC relative mode ?
OVER 77 = Or	PC relative deferred mode?
OR IF	In either case,
SWAP	move operand n to top of the stack.
HERE 2 + -	Compute offset from n to the next instruction address.
SWAP	Put the offset value under addr-field.
ENDIF	
DUP 27 =	PC immediate mode ?
OVER 37 = OR	Or PC absolute mode ?
SWAP	Get addr-field for another test.
177760 AND 60 = OR	Or if it is index addressing mode.

IF , ENDIF I   n any of the three cases, assemble the literal after the instruction code.

;   None of above. The instruction does not need a literal. It is already complete.

: B   --

Modify the instruction code just assembled to the dictionary to make a byte instruction from a cell instruction.

100000   MSB of the byte instruction must be set.

HERE 2 - +!   Toggle the MSB of the instruction code on top of dictionary.

;

B is to be used immediately after an instruction definition like op1 op2 MOV, B to move a byte from op1 to op2. The byte instruction can be defined separately as MOVB,. However, the modifier definition B is more elegant in reducing the number of mnemonic definitions by 25%.

5100 1OP CLR,   5200 1OP INC,   5300 1OP DEC,   5400 1OP NEG,

5500 1OP ADC,   5600 1OP SBC,   5700 1OP TST,   6000 1OP ROR,

6100 1OP ROL,   6200 1OP ASR,   6300 1OP ASL,   6700 1OP SXT,

 6100 1OP JMP,

: ROP   n --

A defining word to define two operand instructions. The source operand can only be a register without mode selection. The destination address field is the lower 6 bits, and the source register is specified by bits 6 to 8.

<BUILDS , DOES>   Make header and store instruction code.

@ ,	When defined instruction is executed, assemble the basic instruction code to the dictionary.
FIXMODE	Fix the destination address field.
DUP	Copy the just completed address field value.
HERE 2 -	Address of the instruction.
DUP >R	Save a copy of this address on the return stack to fix the source register field underneath it on the stack.
ORMODE	Insert the destination address field into the instruction.
,OPERAND	If a literal operand is required, assemble it here.
DUP 7 SWAP U<	The register number must be less than 7 .
IF ." ERR-REG-B" ENDIF	The register number is too big, issue an error message.
100 * R> ORMODE	Justify the source register field value and insert it into the instruction.

;

74000 ROP XOR,   4000 ROP JSR,

: BOP   n --

A defining word used to define branching and conditional branching instructions. This word is included only for completeness since the branchings are not structured. In Forth code definitions, more powerful branching and looping structures should be used, as will be discussed shortly.

<BUILDS , DOES>

@ ,

HERE -   The target address is presummably on data stack.
                   Compute the offset value for branching.

DUP 376 >   If the offset is greater than 376, issue an error message:

IF ." ERR-BR+" . ENDIF   with the out of range offset.

DUP -400 <   If the offset is less than -400, issue an error message:

IF ." ERR-BR-" . ENDIF   with the out of range offset.

2 / 377 AND   The correct offset value is then

HERE 2 = ORMODE   inserted into the instruction code.

;

400 BOP BR,   1000 BOP BNE,   1400 BOP BEQ,   2000 BOP BGE,
400 BOP BLT,   3000 BOP BGT,   3400 BOP BLE,   100000 BOP BPL,
00400 BOP BMI,   101000 BOP BHI,   101400 BOP BLOS, 102000 BOP BVC,
02400 BOP BVS,   103000 BOP BCC,   103400 BOP BCS,   103400 BOP BLO,
103000 BOP BHIS,

: 2OP   n --

A defining word to define two operand instructions.

<BUILDS , DOES>

@ ,

FIXMODE   Fix the mode packet for destination field.

DUP HERE 2 -   Get the address of the instruction to be fixed.

DUP >R   Save a copy of the instruction address on return stack.

ORMODE   Insert the destination field.

,OPERAND   Assemble a literal after the instruction if required.

FIXMODE   Now process the source mode packet.

DUP 100 *   Justify the source field value.

R ORMODE   Insert the source field into the instruction.

,OPERAND   Assemble a literal if required.

HERE R> - 6 =   If there are two literals assembled after the instruction, they are in the wrong order.

IF SWAPOP ENDIF   The two literals have to be swapped.

;

: SWAPOP   --

Swap the two literals after a two operand instruction. If either literal is used for PC addressing, the offset value will have to be adjusted to reflect the swapping.

HERE 2 - @   Push the last literal on the stack.

HERE 6 - @   This is the instruction code itself.

6700 AND 6700 = PC relative mode?

IF 2 + ENDIF   Yes, increment the last literal by 2.

HERE 4 - @   Now work on the first literal.

HERE 6 - @   Get the instruction back again.

67 AND 67 =   Is the destination field also of PC relative mode?

IF 2 - ENDIF   If it is, decrement the branching offset by 2.

HERE 2 - !   Put the first offset last,

HERE 4 - ! ;   and the last offset first.

10000 2OP MOV,   **20000 2OP CMP,**   **30000 2OP BIT,**   **40000 2OP BIC,**

50000 2OP BIS,   **60000 2OP ADD,**   **160000 2OP SUB,**

Two more instructions need to be patched:

: RST,   200 OR , ;

: EMT,   104000 + , ;

The branching instructions are similar to the GOTO statements in high level languages. They are not very useful in promoting modular and structured programming. Therefore, their usage in Forth code definitions is discouraged. Somewhat modified forms of these branch instructions are defined in the assembler to code IF-ELSE-ENDIF and BEGIN-UNTIL types of structures. Although these structures are very similar to the structures used in colon definitions, the functions of these words in the assembler are different. Thus it is a good practice to define them with names ending in commas as all other mnemonic definitions. However, the comma at the end does not imply that an instruction code is always assembled by these special definitions.

The conditional branching instructions are defined as constants to be assembled by the words requiring branching. The notation is reversed from the PDP mnemonics because of this assembling procedure.

1000 IS EQ	1400 IS NE	2000 IS LT	2400 IS GE
3000 IS LE	3400 IS GT	100000 IS MI	101000 IS LOS
101400 IS HI	102000 IS VS	102400 IS VC	103000 IS LO
103400 IS HIS			

: IF,   n -- addr

Take the literal n on stack and assemble it to dictionary as a conditional branching instruction. Leave the address of this branching instruction on the data stack to resolve the branching offset later.

HERE   Address of the branching instruction.

SWAP ,   Assemble the branching instruction to the dictionary.

;

: IPATCH,   addr1 addr2 --

Use the addresses left on the stack to compute the forward branching offset and patch up the instruction assembled by IF, .

OVER -   Byte offset from addr1 to addr2.
                   2 / 1- 377 AND   The 8 bit instruction offset.

SWAP DUP @ Fetch out the branching instruction at addr1 .

ROT OR   Insert the offset into the branching instruction.

SWAP !   Put the completed instruction back.

;

: ENDIF,   addr --

Close the conditional structure in a code definition.

HERE IPATCH, Call on IPATCH, to resolve the forward branching.

;

: ELSE,   addr1 -- addr2

Assemble an unconditional branch instruction at HERE , and patch up the offset field in the instruction assembled by IF, . Leave the address of the current branch instruction on the stack for ENDIF, to resolve.

400 ,   Assemble the BR, instruction to the dictionary.

HERE IPATCH, Patch up the conditional branching instruction at IF, .

HERE 2 -   Leave address of BR, for ELSE, to patch up.

;

: BEGIN,   addr --

HERE   Begin an indefinite loop.
                Push DP on stack for backward branching.

;

: UNTIL,   addr n --

Assemble the conditional branching instruction n to the dictionary, taking addr as the address to branch back to.

,   Assemble n which must be one of the conditional
                branching instruction codes.

HERE 2 -   The address of the above instruction.

SWAP IPATCH, Patch up the offset in the branching instruction.

;

: REPEAT,   addr1 addr2 --

Used in the form: BEGIN, . . . WHILE, . . . REPEAT, inside a code definition. Assemble an unconditional branch instruction pointing to BEGIN, at addr1, and resolve the forward branch offset for WHILE, at addr2 .

HERE   Save the DP pointing to the current BR, instruction.

400 ,   Assemble BR, here.

ROT IPATCH,   Patch the BR, instruction to branch back to BEGIN, at addr1 .

HERE   This is where the conditional branch at WHILE, should
                branch to on false condition.

IPATCH,   Patch up the conditional branch at WHILE, .

;

: WHILE,   n -- addr

Assemble a conditional jump instruction at HERE . Push the address of this instruction addr on the stack for REPEAT, to resolve the forward jump address.

HERE	Push DP to stack.
SWAP	Move n to top of stack, and assemble it literally as an instruction.

;

: C;   addr --

Ending of a code definition started by ENTERCODE .

CURRENT @ CONTEXT !	Restore CONTEXT vocabulary to CURRENT . Thus abandon the ASSEMBLER vocabulary to the current vocabulary where the new code definition was added. The programmer can now test the new definition.
OLDBASE @ BASE !	Restore the old base before assembling.
SP@ 2+ =	Compare the current SP with addr on the stack, IF SMUDGE if they are the same, the stack was not disturbed. Restore the smudged header to complete the new definition. Otherwise, issue an error message.

ELSE ." CODE ERROR, STACK DEPTH CHANGED"

ENDIF

;

: NEXT,   --

The address interpreter returning execution process to the colon definition which calls the code definition. This must be the last word in a code definition before C; .

IP)+ W MOV,   Move the contents of IP to W. IP is incremented by 2.

W @)+ JMP,   Jump to execute the instruction sequence pointed to by the contents of W. W is incremented by 2, pointing to the parameter field of the word to be executed.

;

FORTH DEFINITIONS

The assembler vocabulary is now completed. Return to the FORTH trunk vocabulary by setting both CONTEXT and CURRENT to FORTH .

DECIMAL   Restore decimal base. The base was changed to octal when entering the a process of creating the assembler.

14.3.   8080 ASSEMBLER

The assembler is usually defined in an independent vocabulary separated from the trunk FORTH vocabulary and other vocabularies. To generate the ASSEMBLER vocabulary and to make some modifications in the FORTH vocabulary, the following words must be executed. These words are commands to setup the ASSEMBLER vocabulary. This 8080 Assembler was authored by John Cassidy, who also built the 8080 figForth Model.

HEX   All 8080 codes will be represented in hexadecimal base.

VOCABULARY ASSEMBLER   Create a new vocabulary for assembler.

IMMEDIATE   Vocabulary must be of IMMEDIATE type to be used within colon definitions.

' ASSEMBLER CFA   Get the code field address of ASSEMBLER definition, and

' ;CODE 0A + !   patch up the code in ;CODE . This is to replace the word SMUDGE with ASSEMBLER , so that the codes following ;CODE can be understood in the context of the assembler.
The function of SMUDGE is deferred to the end of the code sequence in C; .

: CODE   --

A more fully developed definition to start a code definition with error checking.

?EXEC   If not executing, issue an error message.

CREATE   Create a new dictionary header with the following name.

[COMPILE]   Compile the next IMMEDIATE word.

ASSEMBLER   Switch the CONTEXT to ASSEMBLER vocabulary to search assembly mnemonics first before the current vocabulary.

!CSP   Store current stack pointer in CSP for later error checking.

; IMMEDIATE

: C;   --

Ending of a new code definition. Check for error and restore the smudged header.

CURRENT @ CONTEXT !   At the beginning of assembly, CONTEXT was switched to ASSEMBLER, to search for the assembler mnemonics. After the code definition is completed, CONTEXT must be restored to CURRENT vocabulary to continue program development or testing.

?EXEC   If not executing, issue an error message.

?CSP   If the data stack was disturbed, issue an error message.

; IMMEDIATE

: LABEL   --

Define a subroutine which can be called by the assembler CALL instruction. It is not necessary in Forth.

?EXEC

0 VARIABLE   Subroutine header is defined as a variable with a
dummy

                value 0. When the name is executed, the

address of its

                parameter field will be put on the stack to be

used by the

                CALLing instruction.

SMUDGE   Smudge the header as usual.

-2 ALLOT   Backup the dictionary pointer to overwrite the
                dummy 0 with the subroutine.

[COMPILE] ASSEMBLER   Get the assembler to process the
                mnemonics following.

!CSP   Store SP for error checking.

; IMMEDIATE

: 8*   n -- n*8

Multiply top of stack by 8.

DUP + DUP + DUP + ;   Faster than doing real multiplication on an 8080.

ASSEMBLER DEFINITIONS

Set both the CONTEXT and CURRENT vocabularies to ASSEMBLER . Now, all subsequent definitions are put into the ASSEMBLER vocabulary to be referenced by CODE and ;CODE . The definitions up to this point went into the FORTH vocabulary.

: IS   n --

CONSTANT ;   Shorthand of CONSTANT .

Following are register name definitions:

0 IS B   1 IS C   2 IS D   3 IS E   4 IS H   5 IS L   6 IS M

7 IS A   6 IS PSW   6 IS SP   2A28 IS NEXT

In 8080 fig-Forth, NEXT was defined as a code routine starting at address 2A28 in memory. With NEXT thus defined as a constant, NEXT JMP should be the last instruction in a code definition before C; .

: 1MI   n --

A defining word to create single byte 8080 instructions without operands. MI stands for machine instruction.

<BUILDS   Create a header with the name following.

C,   Store instruction code on the stack to the parameter field.

DOES>   The following words are to be executed when the newly defined mnemonic name is executed during assembly.

C@ C,   Fetch the instruction code stored in the parameter field and assemble it into the dictionary as a byte literal.

;

The following single byte instructions are defined by 1MI .

76 1MI HLT	**07 1MI RLC**	**0F 1MI RRC**	**17 1MI RAL**
1F 1MI RAR	**C9 1MI RET**	**D8 1MI RC**	**D0 1MI RNC**
C8 1MI RZ	**C0 1MI RNZ**	**F0 1MI RP**	**F8 1MI RM**
E8 1MI RPE	**E0 1MI RPO**	**2F 1MI CMA**	**37 1MI STC**
3F 1MI CMC	**27 1MI DAA**	**FB 1MI EI**	**F3 1MI DI**
00 1MI NOP	**E9 1MI PCHL**	**F9 1MI SPHL**	**E3 XTHL**
EB 1MI XCHG			

: 2MI   n --

A defining word to define 8080A instructions with a source operand. The source field is the least significant 3 bits.

<BUILDS C, DOES>   Create a header for the mnemonic name following.
                                Store the instruction code in the parameter field.

C@ + C,   When the mnemonic defined is executed, the code value
            is pulled out from the parameter field, the number
            representing the source register on the stack is added
            to the code and the completed instruction is assembled
            to the dictionary.

;

The following 8080 instructions are defined by 2MI :

```
80 2MI ADD     88 2MI ADC     90 2MI SUB     98 2MI SBB

A0 2MI ANA     A8 2MI XRA     B0 2MI ORA     B8 2MI CMP
```

: 3MI   n --

A defining word to define 8080 instructions with destination register specified in the bits 3, 4, and 5.

<BUILDS C, DOES>

C@	When the mnemonic is executed during assembly, the basic code value is fetched from the parameter field.
SWAP	The operand's register number on the stack is swapped over the code value, and
8*	multiplied by 8 to line up with the destination field.
+ C,	Add the register number to the instruction and assemble it.
;	

Following instructions are defined by 3MI :

```
04 3MI INR     05 3MI DCR     C7 3MI RST     C5 3MI PUSH

C1 3MI POP     09 3MI DAD     02 3MI STAX    0A 3MI LDAX

03 3MI INX     0B 3MI DCX
```

: 4MI   n --

A defining word to define 8080 instruction with an immediate byte value following the instruction code.

<BUILDS C, DOES>

C@ C, C,   The instruction code is fetched from the parameter field and assembled into the dictionary, and the byte value given on the stack is assembled following the instruction code.

;

Examples are:

    C6 4MI ADI   **CE 4MI ACI**   **D6 4MI SUI**   **DE 4MI SBI**

    E6 4MI ANI   **EE 4MI XRI**   **F6 4MI ORI**   **FE 4MI CPI**

    DB 4MI IN   **D3 4MI OUT**

: 5MI   **n --**

A defining word to define 8080 instruction taking a 16 bit value as an operand, either as an address or as an immediate value for operations.

<BUILDS C, DOES>

C@ C,   When the defined mnemonic is executed, the instruction code is assembled to the dictionary.
The number on the stack is assembled after the instruction.

;

Examples are:

    C3 5MI JMP   **CD 5MI CALL 3 2 5MI STA**   **3A 5MI LDA**

    22 5MI SHLD   **2A 5MI LHLD**

The 8080 MOV instruction needs two operands to specify the source and destination registers for data movements. The two register numbers are pushed on the data stack for the MOV definition to pick up and assemble as one instruction code. The MVI and LXI instructions behave similarly.

: MOV   b1 b2 --

Assemble a MOV instruction to the dictionary with b1 representing source register and b2 destination register.

8*   b2*8 is the destination field.

40   Basic code for a MOV instruction.

+ +   Add the source and destination fields to the instruction.

C,   Assemble to dictionary.

;

: MVI   b1 b2 --

Assemble a MVI instruction to dictionary, with b2 specifying the destination field and b1 the immediate byte value following the instruction.

8*   Destination field.

6   Basic MVI instruction code.

+ C,   Assemble the instruction.

C,   Assemble the immediate byte value after the instruction.

;

: LXI   n b --

Assemble a LXI instruction with b specifying the destination register pair, and n as a two byte immediate value to be loaded into the register pair.

8* 1+ C, Assemble the LXI instruction.

,   Assemble the two byte immediate value after the instruction.

;

The foregoing discussion covers most of the 8080 instruction set with the exception of conditional jump instructions. The reason is that the conditional jumps are used to construct the more structured definitions like IF-ELSE-ENDIF and BEGIN-UNTIL. The non-structured jump instructions such as CALL, RET, conditional CALL's and RET's are defined in the assembler for completeness.

Subroutines are better defined as independent colon or code definitions. The short jumps in code definitions are implemented in the following way. Instead of the regular conditional jump instruction, a set of Forth words are defined to be used with the conditional structures:

C2 IS 0=   **D2 IS CS**   **E2 IS PE**   **F2 IS 0<**

: NOT   b1 -- b2

Negate the conditional b1 to reverse the jumping condition.

8 + ;   The byte value b2 is to be assembled by the instruction
              IF , etc., to effect conditional branching.

: IF   b -- addr 2

Assemble the conditional b into the dictionary. Leave on the stack the current dictionary pointer to resolve later the forward branching address, and a flag 2 for error checking.

C,   Assemble the conditional b.

HERE   Push current DP to stack as addr.

0 ,   Assemble a dummy 0 here for forward jumping. The address will be resolved by ELSE or ENDIF .

2   Flag for error checking.

;

: ENDIF   addr n --

Terminate an IF-ELSE-ENDIF structure in a code definition.   Check n for error. Use addr to resolve the forward jumping address at IF or ELSE .

2 ?PAIRS   If n is not 2, issue an error message.

HERE SWAP !   Store the current DP to addr after IF or ELSE to complete the conditional structure.

;

: ELSE   addr1 n -- addr2 2

Start a false clause in a code definition. Resolve the forward branching at addr1 and leave the present address addr2 and a flag on the stack to be used by ENDIF .

2 ?PAIRS   If n is not 2, issue an error message.

C3 IF   Use IF to assemble a unconditional jump instruction (C3) to the dictionary, and also leave addr2 and 2 on the stack.

ROT   Get addr1 to top of stack.

SWAP   The stack is now addr2 addr1 n2 .

ENDIF   Take n2 and addr1 from top of the stack to resolve the jump address at IF .

2   n2 the flag.

;

: BEGIN   -- addr 1

Start an indefinite loop such as

BEGIN . . . UNTIL ,

 BEGIN ... WHILE ... REPEAT ,

or

BEGIN ... AGAIN .

HERE	Leave current DP on stack for backward branching from the end of the loop.
1	Flag for error checking.
;	

: UNTIL   addr n b --

End of an indefinite loop. Assemble a conditional jump instruction b and address addr of BEGIN for backward branching.

SWAP	Get n to top of the stack for error checking.
1 ?PAIRS	If n is not 1 , issue an error message.
C,	Assemble b literally as a conditional jump instruction.
,	Assemble the address addr of BEGIN for branching.
;	

: AGAIN   addr n --

End of an infinite loop. Assemble an unconditional jump instruction to branch backward to addr .

1 ?PAIRS   Check n for error.

C3 C,   Assemble the JMP instruction,

,   with the address addr .

;

: WHILE   b -- addr 4

Abort an infinite loop from the middle inside the loop. Assemble a conditional jump instruction b , and leave the DP and a flag on the stack for REPEAT to resolve the backward jump address.

Used in the form:

BEGIN . . . WHILE . . . REPEAT

IF   Use IF to do the dirty work.

2+   The flag left by IF is 2. Change it to 4 for REPEAT to verify.

;

: REPEAT   addr1 n1 addr2 n2 --

Assemble JMP addr1 to dictionary to close the loop from BEGIN . Resolve forward jump address at addr2 as required by WHILE .

>R >R   Get addr2 and n2 out of way.

AGAIN   Let AGAIN assemble the backward jump.

R> R> 2-   Bring back addr2 and n2. Change n2 back to 2.

ENDIF   Check error. Resolve jump address for WHILE.

;

FORTH DEFINITIONS

The whole ASSEMBLER vocabulary is now completed.   Restore the CONTEXT and CURRENT vocabularies to the trunk FORTH vocabulary for normal programming activity.

DECIMAL   Restore base from hexadecimal.

####

eBook material re-formatted for Print Book

Juergen Pintaske – ExMark – June 2020

150

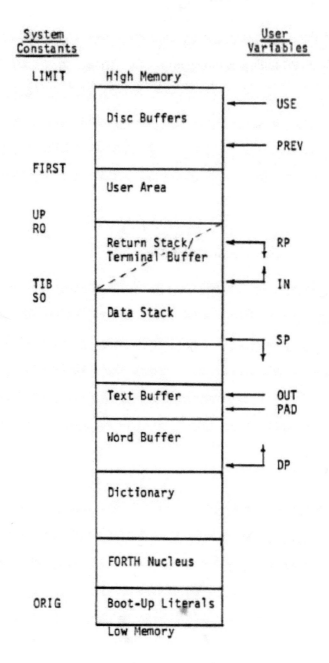

Figure 1: Memory Map of a typical Forth System

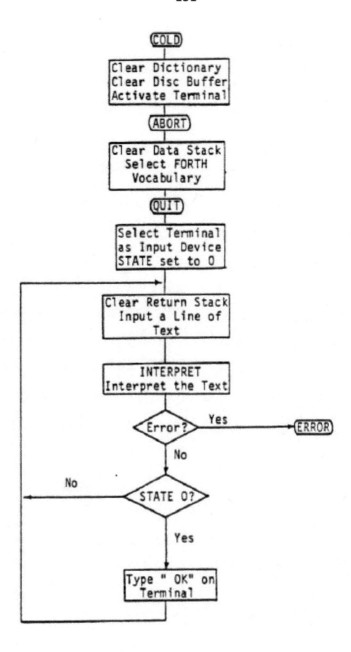

Figure 2: The Forth Loop

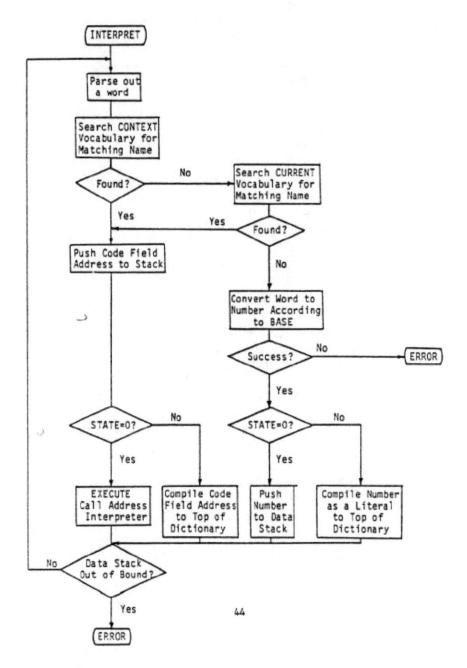

Figure 3: The Interpreter Loop

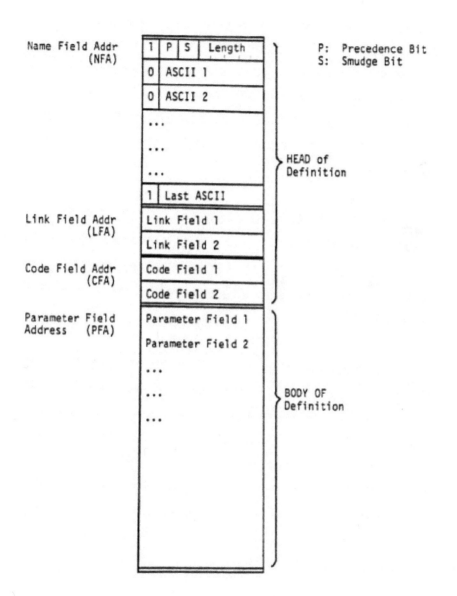

Figure 4: Structure of a Definition

Fig. 5. Error Handling

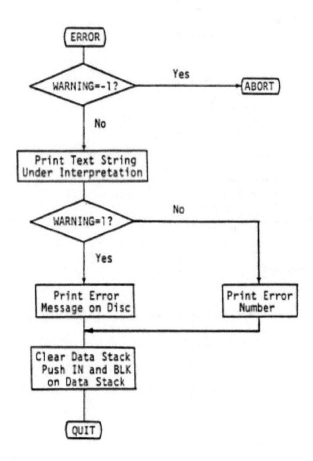

Figure 5: Error Handling

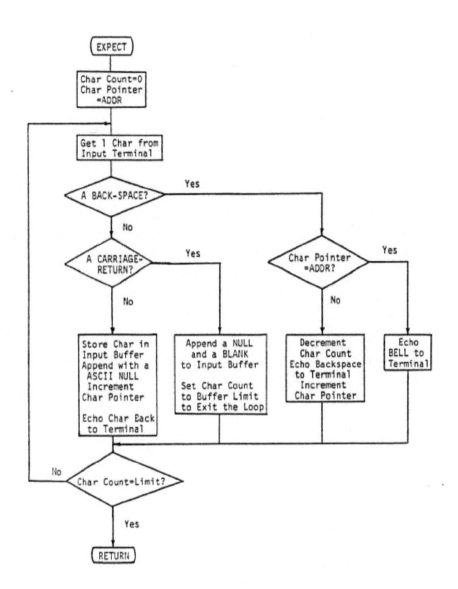

Figure 6: Expect

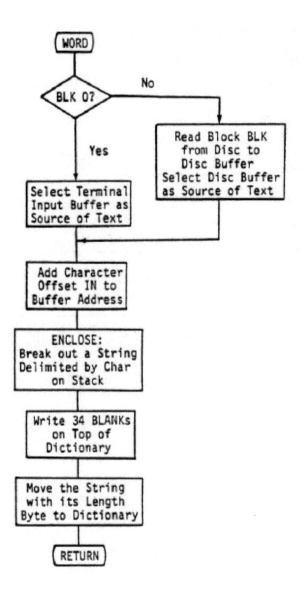

Figure 7: Word

Fig. 8.   Numeric Conversion

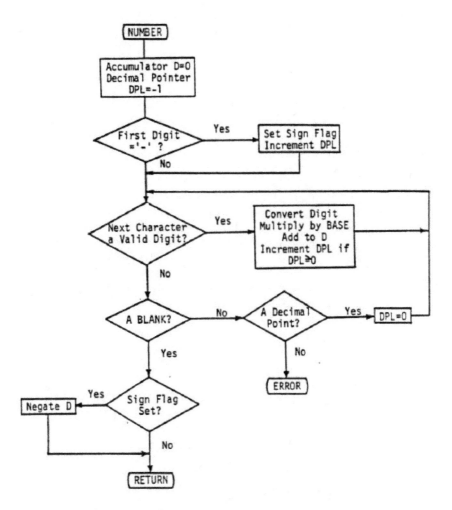

Figure 8: Numeric Conversion

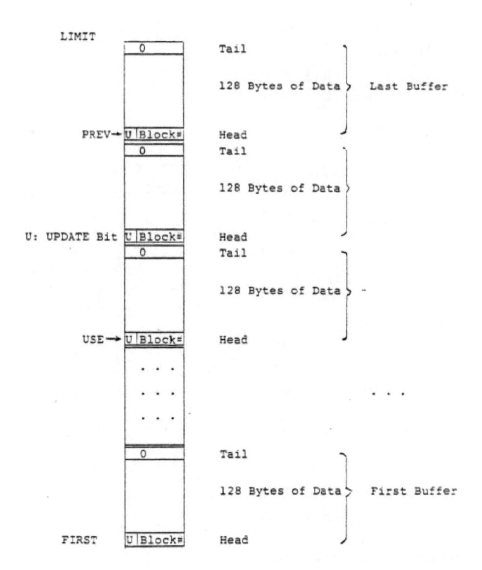

Figure 9: Disk Buffers

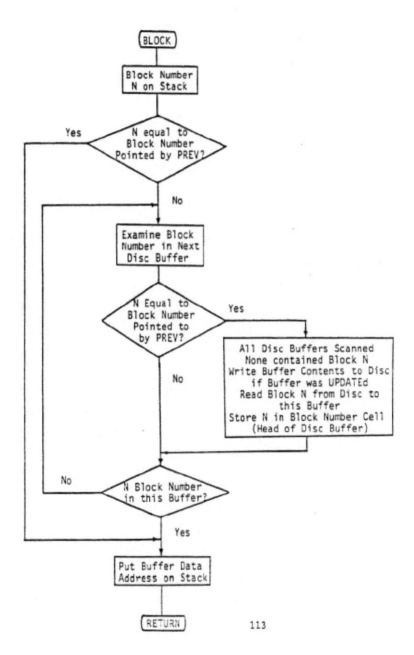

Figure 10: Block

```
: IMMEDIATE  (---)
        LATEST 40H TOGGLE ;
```

A LOADER BLOCK OR SCREEN COULD BE THE FOLLOWING

36 LOAD 37 LOAD 41 LOAD 42 LOAD 19 LOAD

THIS LINE OF TEXT WOULD BE IN SAY, SCREEN 87, SO ALL
YOU NEED TO TYPE NOW WOULD BE 87 LOAD

Figure 11: Immediate - Handwritten addition in the original manual

Testing the FIG-Forth
using the original CDP1802 FIG-Forth running on an FPGA via an 1802 processor core in VHDL

The "remote" teamwork of 3 people who have not met yet in person:

Juergen Pintaske   – to organise and drive it
Scott Baker   – owns quite a few cores and the 1802
Steve Teal   – was working on a CDP1802 implementation

Just getting this eBook formatted and published was not enough. We wanted to be sure, that it all still works.

The hardware would require a board, an interface to the PC, but we wanted to find a simple way, so others can replicate the experience.

In another project, we try to bring back the CDP1802 as VHDL in FPGA. This would need as well a board to run it on.

And suddenly it all fell into place.

The choice was a Lattice Semiconductor ICE 8k board. 8000 LUTs of logic is more and enough for our project. The 1802 just needs about 1000 LUTs.

As well the Flash Memory is sufficient.

And we have 16k of RAM for the FIG-Forth.

The interface to the PC is part of the board, so the USB cable we need already comes with the board.

And the serial interface runs via the USB cable. So no additional connections.

On the PC side a Terminal function is sufficient, we used Teraterm.

It was a very nice surprise when I received the programmed board from Steve, connect to the PC, start the terminal software and see the result:

```
COM41:115200baud - Tera Term VT
File  Edit  Setup  Control  Window  Help
   OK
   OK
   OK
   OK
   OK
: hello ." HELLO FORTH WORLD FIG FORTH ON 1802 IP " ;   OK
HELLO HELLO  ? MSG # 0
hello HELLO FORTH WORLD FIG FORTH ON 1802 IP   OK
: test ." starting to test - juergen pintaske exmark " ;   OK
test starting to test - juergen pintaske exmark   OK
hello test  HELLO FORTH WORLD FIG FORTH ON 1802 IP starting to test - juergen pintaske exmark   OK
```

More to be tested over the next couple of months. The Image of the system will be made available so others can replicate the system using the same board – not clear yet where, but try www.Forth-eV.de or Google.

Hex Dump of the FIG-Forth running in the FPGA RAM

From 0000 – 163F Hex, the rest up to 8k is free for Forth programs:

```
0000 71 00 61 01 63 1D F8 00 B3 F8 5E A3 F8 2F B2 F8
0010 FF A2 D3 00 00 00 00 00 00 00 00 00 00 00 00 00
0020 00 00 00 00 00 00 00 00 00 00 00 00 00 00 00 00
0030 00 00 00 00 00 00 00 00 00 00 00 00 00 00 00 00
0040 00 00 00 00 00 00 00 00 00 00 00 00 00 00 00 00
0050 00 00 00 00 00 00 00 00 00 00 00 00 00 00 C4 C0
0060 19 00 C4 C0 19 15 07 0A 00 01 18 BF 00 08 20 00
0070 1F 00 1F FF 1F 80 00 1F 00 00 19 3D 19 3D 0F 6A
0080 83 4C 49 D4 00 00 00 88 19 19 4A 59 19 4A 59 29
0090 DC D3 4A BB 4A AB 4B B3 4B A3 30 91 87 45 58 45
00A0 43 55 54 C5 00 80 00 A8 49 BB 09 AB 29 29 29 1C
00B0 1C 1C 1C DC 86 42 52 41 4E 43 C8 00 9C 00 BF 4A
00C0 52 4A AA 02 BA DC 87 30 42 52 41 4E 43 C8 00 B4
00D0 00 D2 49 3A DD 09 3A DD 29 29 29 30 BF 1A 1A 29
00E0 29 29 DC 86 28 4C 4F 4F 50 A9 00 C6 00 EE 12 92
00F0 B8 B7 82 A8 A7 22 08 FC 01 58 18 08 7C 00 C4 C4

0100 58 18 E7 48 F5 17 08 75 FA 80 32 13 4A 52 0A AA
0110 02 BA DC 1A 1A 12 12 12 12 DC 87 28 2B 4C 4F 4F
0120 50 A9 00 E3 01 26 12 92 B8 B7 82 A8 A7 22 E9 19
0130 08 F4 58 18 29 08 74 58 09 FE 29 29 33 40 30 01
0140 18 E7 48 F7 17 08 77 30 08 84 28 44 4F A9 01 1A
0150 01 52 29 29 E2 49 73 49 73 49 73 09 73 29 29 29
0160 29 29 DC 85 44 49 47 49 D4 01 49 01 6D E9 29 09
0170 FF 30 3B 88 FF 11 33 7C FF F9 33 88 FC 0A 59 19
0180 19 F7 33 86 29 DC 29 29 F8 00 73 59 DC 86 28 46
0190 49 4E 44 A9 01 63 01 98 29 29 49 B8 49 A8 49 B7
01A0 09 A7 29 29 E7 07 52 48 F3 FA 3F 3A D3 17 48 F3
01B0 FE 3A D4 7E 32 AD 47 FA 80 32 B6 E9 87 FC 04 73
01C0 97 7C 00 59 19 19 F8 00 59 19 02 59 19 F8 FF 59
01D0 19 73 DC 17 47 FA 80 32 D4 07 3A E7 17 07 27 3A
01E0 E7 F8 00 59 29 59 DC 47 52 07 A7 02 B7 09 A8 29
01F0 49 B8 30 A4 87 45 4E 43 4C 4F 53 C5 01 8D 02 00

0200 29 29 49 B8 49 A8 19 F8 00 A7 09 52 E2 08 F7 3A
0210 15 18 17 30 0D 87 59 B7 19 F8 00 59 19 19 59 19
0220 08 32 2A F7 32 38 18 17 30 20 87 E9 59 97 F7 3A
0230 32 17 87 29 29 59 19 DC 17 87 59 27 30 32 85 43
0240 4D 4F 56 C5 01 F4 02 48 49 FC 01 B7 09 A7 27 29
```

```
0250 29 29 9A 52 22 8A 52 49 BA 09 AA 29 29 29 49 B8
0260 09 A8 29 29 29 97 32 6E 48 5A 1A 27 30 65 42 AA
0270 02 BA DC 82 55 AA 02 3E 02 7A E9 F8 00 A7 B7 F8
0280 10 52 87 FE A7 97 7E B7 19 09 7E 73 09 7E 59 3B
0290 A0 29 87 F4 A7 29 97 74 B7 19 19 19 F8 00 74 73
02A0 02 FF 01 3A 81 29 87 73 97 59 19 19 DC 82 55 AF
02B0 02 73 02 B4 E9 29 29 49 B7 09 A7 29 29 49 FE 19
02C0 73 29 29 49 7E 19 59 19 F8 10 A8 87 7E A7 97 7E
02D0 B7 19 19 87 F7 B8 29 97 77 3B DE B7 98 A7 29 09
02E0 7E 73 09 7E 59 19 28 88 3A CB 29 30 A5 83 41 4E
02F0 C4 02 AD 02 F5 89 A8 99 B8 28 E8 19 09 F2 73 29

0300 09 F2 58 29 29 DC 82 4F D2 02 ED 03 0D 89 A8 99
0310 B8 28 E8 19 09 F1 73 29 09 F1 58 29 29 DC 83 58
0320 4F D2 03 06 03 26 89 A8 99 B8 28 E8 19 09 F3 73
0330 29 09 F3 58 29 29 DC 83 53 50 C0 03 1E 03 3F 99
0340 52 89 19 19 19 59 29 02 59 DC 83 53 50 A1 03 37
0350 03 52 8D FC 06 A8 9D 7C 00 B8 48 B9 08 A9 DC 83
0360 52 50 A1 03 4A 03 67 8D FC 08 A8 9D 7C 00 B8 48
0370 B2 08 A2 DC 82 3B D3 03 5F 03 7B 12 42 AA 02 BA
0380 DC 85 4C 45 41 56 C5 03 74 03 8B 92 B8 82 A8 18
0390 48 18 58 28 48 18 58 DC 82 3E D2 03 81 03 9F E2
03A0 49 73 09 73 29 29 29 DC 82 52 BE 03 98 03 AF 19
03B0 19 19 12 42 59 29 02 59 DC 81 D2 03 A8 03 BF 82
03C0 A8 92 B8 18 19 19 19 48 59 29 08 59 DC 82 30 BD
03D0 03 B9 03 D4 49 3A DE 09 3A DE F8 01 30 E0 F8 00
03E0 59 29 F8 00 59 DC 82 30 BC 03 CD 03 ED 49 FE 33
03F0 DA 30 DE 81 AB 03 E6 03 F9 89 A8 99 B8 28 E8 19

0400 09 F4 73 29 09 74 58 29 29 DC 85 4D 49 4E 55 D3
0410 03 F3 04 14 FF 00 19 09 FB FF 7C 00 59 29 09 FB
0420 FF 7C 00 59 DC 82 44 AB 04 0A 04 2C 89 FF 05 A8
0430 99 7F 00 B8 29 E8 09 F4 73 29 09 74 58 18 18 18
0440 19 19 19 09 74 73 29 09 74 58 29 29 29 29 DC 86
0450 44 4D 49 4E 55 D3 04 25 04 5A E9 29 09 FB FF FC
0460 01 73 09 FB FF 7C 00 59 19 19 30 16 84 4F 56 45
0470 D2 04 4F 04 75 29 29 49 19 19 19 59 29 29 29 49
0480 19 19 19 59 29 DC 84 44 52 4F D0 04 6C 04 8F 29
0490 29 DC 84 53 57 41 D0 04 86 04 9B 89 A8 99 B8 28
04A0 08 52 19 09 58 02 59 29 28 08 52 09 58 02 59 DC
04B0 83 44 55 D0 04 92 04 B8 49 19 59 29 49 19 59 29
04C0 DC 82 2B A1 04 B0 04 C8 49 B8 09 A8 29 29 18 E8
04D0 09 F4 73 29 09 74 58 29 29 DC 86 54 4F 47 47 4C
```

```
04E0  C5 04 C1 04 E5 19 09 A7 29 29 29 49 B8 09 A8 E8
04F0  87 F3 58 29 30 D7 81 C0 04 DA 04 FC 49 B8 09 A8

0500  29 48 59 19 08 59 29 DC 82 43 C0 04 F6 05 0F 49
0510  B8 09 A8 08 59 29 F8 00 59 DC 81 A1 05 08 05 20
0520  49 B8 09 A8 29 29 29 49 58 18 09 58 29 29 29 DC
0530  82 43 A1 05 1A 05 37 49 B8 09 A8 29 29 09 58 29
0540  29 29 DC 84 45 4D 49 D4 05 30 05 C2 06 DB 05 52
0550  03 79 05 54 49 B8 09 A8 29 29 29 18 08 FC 01 58
0560  28 08 7C 00 58 E2 6B FE 3B 65 E9 19 62 29 29 29
0570  29 DC 83 4B 45 D9 05 43 05 7A E9 60 60 60 6B F6
0580  3B 7E 6A FA 7F 59 29 F8 00 59 DC 89 3F 54 45 52
0590  4D 49 4E 41 CC 05 72 05 99 E9 60 60 60 6B FA 08
05A0  73 6A F8 00 59 DC 82 43 D2 05 8B 05 AD E2 6B FE
05B0  3B AE F8 0D 52 62 22 6B FE 3B B7 F8 0A 52 62 22
05C0  E9 DC 9A 52 22 8A 52 22 9B BA 8B AA DC 19 19 9B
05D0  59 19 8B 59 29 DC 19 19 4B 59 19 4B 59 29 DC 19
05E0  19 E9 4B 59 19 4B 59 8D F4 73 9D 74 59 DC 81 B0
05F0  05 A6 05 D6 00 00 81 B1 05 EE 05 D6 00 01 81 B2

0600  05 F6 05 D6 00 02 82 42 CC 05 FE 05 D6 00 20 83
0610  43 2F CC 06 06 05 D6 00 40 85 46 49 52 53 D4 06
0620  0F 05 D6 40 00 85 4C 49 4D 49 D4 06 19 05 D6 6C
0630  2C 85 42 2F 42 55 C6 06 25 05 D6 04 00 85 42 2F
0640  53 43 D2 06 31 05 D6 00 01 86 4F 52 49 47 49 CE
0650  06 3D 05 D6 00 5E 87 2B 4F 52 49 47 49 CE 06 49
0660  05 C2 06 52 03 F7 03 79 82 53 B0 06 56 05 DF 00
0670  06 82 52 B0 06 68 05 DF 00 08 83 54 49 C2 06 71
0680  05 DF 00 0A 85 57 49 44 54 C8 06 7A 05 DF 00 0C
0690  87 57 41 52 4E 49 4E C7 06 84 05 DF 00 0E 85 46
06A0  45 4E 43 C5 06 90 05 DF 00 10 82 44 D0 06 9E 05
06B0  DF 00 12 88 56 4F 43 2D 4C 49 4E CB 06 AA 05 DF
06C0  00 14 83 42 4C CB 06 B3 05 DF 00 16 82 49 CE 06
06D0  C2 05 DF 00 18 83 4F 55 D4 06 CC 05 DF 00 1A 83
06E0  53 43 D2 06 D5 05 DF 00 1C 86 4F 46 46 53 45 D4
06F0  06 DF 05 DF 00 1E 87 43 4F 4E 54 45 58 D4 06 E9

0700  05 DF 00 20 87 43 55 52 52 45 4E D4 06 F6 05 DF
0710  00 22 85 53 54 41 54 C5 07 04 05 DF 00 24 84 42
0720  41 53 C5 07 12 05 DF 00 26 83 44 50 CC 07 1E 05
0730  DF 00 28 83 46 4C C4 07 29 05 DF 00 2A 83 43 53
0740  D0 07 33 05 DF 00 2C 82 52 A3 07 3D 05 DF 00 2E
0750  83 48 4C C4 07 47 05 DF 00 30 82 44 D6 07 50 05
```

```
0760 DF 00 32 82 31 AB 07 5A 05 C2 05 FA 03 F7 03 79
0770 82 32 AB 07 63 05 C2 06 02 03 F7 03 79 84 48 45
0780 52 C5 07 70 05 C2 06 AF 04 FA 03 79 85 41 4C 4C
0790 4F D4 07 7D 05 C2 06 AF 04 C6 03 79 81 AC 07 8C
07A0 05 C2 07 84 05 1E 06 02 07 94 03 79 82 43 AC 07
07B0 9C 05 C2 07 84 05 35 05 FA 07 94 03 79 81 AD 07
07C0 AC 05 C2 04 12 03 F7 03 79 81 BD 07 BD 05 C2 07
07D0 C1 03 D2 03 79 81 BC 07 C9 05 C2 07 C1 03 EB 03
07E0 79 81 BE 07 D5 05 C2 04 99 07 D9 03 79 83 52 4F
07F0 D4 07 E1 05 C2 03 9D 04 99 03 AD 04 99 03 79 85

0800 53 50 41 43 C5 07 ED 05 C2 06 0B 05 4A 03 79 84
0810 2D 44 55 D0 07 FF 05 C2 04 B6 00 D0 08 20 04 B6
0820 03 79 88 54 52 41 56 45 52 53 C5 08 0F 05 C2 04
0830 99 04 73 03 F7 00 86 00 7F 04 73 05 0D 07 D9 00
0840 D0 08 31 04 99 04 8D 03 79 86 4C 41 54 45 53 D4
0850 08 22 05 C2 07 0E 04 FA 04 FA 03 79 83 4C 46 C1
0860 08 49 05 C2 00 86 00 04 07 C1 03 79 83 43 46 C1
0870 08 5C 05 C2 06 02 07 C1 03 79 83 4E 46 C1 08 6C
0880 05 C2 00 86 00 05 07 C1 00 86 FF FF 08 2D 03 79
0890 83 50 46 C1 08 7A 05 C2 05 FA 08 2D 00 86 00 05
08A0 03 F7 03 79 84 21 43 53 D0 08 90 05 C2 03 3D 07
08B0 43 05 1E 03 79 86 3F 45 52 52 4F D2 08 A4 05 C2
08C0 04 99 00 D0 08 CC 0C E5 00 BD 08 CE 04 8D 03 79
08D0 85 3F 43 4F 4D D0 08 B5 05 C2 07 1A 04 FA 03 D2
08E0 00 86 00 11 08 BE 03 79 85 3F 45 58 45 C3 08 D0
08F0 05 C2 07 1A 04 FA 00 86 00 12 08 BE 03 79 86 3F

0900 50 41 49 52 D3 08 E8 05 C2 07 C1 00 86 00 13 08
0910 BE 03 79 84 3F 43 53 D0 08 FE 05 C2 03 3D 07 43
0920 04 FA 07 C1 00 86 00 14 08 BE 03 79 88 3F 4C 4F
0930 41 44 49 4E C7 09 13 05 C2 06 C8 04 FA 03 D2 00
0940 86 00 16 08 BE 03 79 87 43 4F 4D 50 49 4C C5 09
0950 2C 05 C2 08 D8 03 AD 04 B6 07 75 03 9D 04 FA 07
0960 A0 03 79 C1 DB 09 47 05 C2 05 F2 07 1A 05 1E 03
0970 79 81 DD 09 63 05 C2 00 86 00 C0 07 1A 05 1E 03
0980 79 86 53 4D 55 44 47 C5 09 71 05 C2 08 52 00 86
0990 00 20 04 E3 03 79 83 48 45 D8 09 81 05 C2 00 86
09A0 00 10 07 25 05 1E 03 79 87 44 45 43 49 4D 41 CC
09B0 09 96 05 C2 00 86 00 0A 07 25 05 1E 03 79 87 28
09C0 3B 43 4F 44 45 A9 09 A8 05 C2 03 AD 08 52 08 96
09D0 08 72 05 1E 03 79 C5 3B 43 4F 44 C5 09 BE 05 C2
09E0 09 1A 09 51 09 C8 09 67 09 8A 03 79 85 43 4F 55
```

```
09F0 4E D4 09 D6 05 C2 04 B6 07 68 04 99 05 0D 03 79

0A00 84 54 59 50 C5 09 EC 05 C2 08 16 00 D0 0A 25 04
0A10 73 03 F7 04 99 01 50 03 BD 05 0D 05 4A 00 EC 0A
0A20 17 00 BD 0A 27 04 8D 03 79 89 2D 54 52 41 49 4C
0A30 49 4E C7 0A 00 05 C2 04 B6 05 F2 01 50 04 73 04
0A40 73 03 F7 05 FA 07 C1 05 0D 06 0B 07 C1 00 D0 0A
0A50 57 03 89 00 BD 0A 5B 05 FA 07 C1 00 EC 0A 3D 03
0A60 79 84 28 2E 22 A9 0A 29 05 C2 03 BD 09 F4 04 B6
0A70 07 68 03 AD 03 F7 03 9D 0A 07 03 79 86 45 58 50
0A80 45 43 D4 0A 61 05 C2 04 73 03 F7 04 73 01 50 05
0A90 78 04 B6 00 86 00 0E 06 60 04 FA 07 CD 00 D0 0A
0AA0 BF 04 8D 00 86 00 08 04 73 03 BD 07 CD 04 B6 03
0AB0 AD 06 02 07 C1 03 F7 03 9D 07 C1 00 BD 0A E5 04
0AC0 B6 00 86 00 0D 07 CD 00 D0 0A D7 03 89 04 8D 06
0AD0 0B 05 F2 00 BD 0A D9 04 B6 03 BD 05 35 05 F2 03
0AE0 BD 07 68 05 1E 05 4A 00 EC 0A 8F 04 8D 03 79 85
0AF0 51 55 45 52 D9 0A 7C 05 C2 06 80 04 FA 00 86 00

0B00 50 0A 85 05 F2 06 D1 05 1E 03 79 C1 80 0A EF 05
0B10 C2 06 C8 04 FA 00 D0 0B 3F 05 FA 06 C8 04 C6 05
0B20 F2 06 D1 05 1E 06 C8 04 FA 00 86 00 07 02 F3 03
0B30 D2 00 D0 0B 3B 08 F0 03 AD 04 8D 00 BD 0B 43 03
0B40 AD 04 8D 03 79 84 46 49 4C CC 0B 0B 05 C2 04 99
0B50 03 9D 04 73 05 35 04 B6 07 68 03 AD 05 FA 07 C1
0B60 02 46 03 79 85 45 52 41 53 C5 0B 45 05 C2 05 F2
0B70 0B 4C 03 79 86 42 4C 41 4E 4B D3 0B 64 05 C2 06
0B80 0B 0B 4C 03 79 84 48 4F 4C C4 0B 74 05 C2 00 86
0B90 FF FF 07 56 04 C6 07 56 04 FA 05 35 03 79 83 50
0BA0 41 C4 0B 85 05 C2 07 84 00 86 00 44 03 F7 03 79
0BB0 84 57 4F 52 C4 0B 9E 05 C2 06 C8 04 FA 00 D0 0B
0BC0 CB 06 C8 04 FA 16 0A 00 BD 0B CF 06 80 04 FA 06
0BD0 D1 04 FA 03 F7 04 99 01 FE 07 84 00 86 00 22 0B
0BE0 7D 06 D1 04 C6 04 73 07 C1 03 9D 03 BD 07 84 05
0BF0 35 03 F7 07 84 07 68 03 AD 02 46 03 79 88 28 4E

0C00 55 4D 42 45 52 A9 0B B0 05 C2 07 68 04 B6 03 9D
0C10 05 0D 07 25 04 FA 01 6B 00 D0 0C 46 04 99 07 25
0C20 04 FA 02 78 04 8D 07 F3 07 25 04 FA 02 78 04 2A
0C30 07 2F 04 FA 07 68 00 D0 0C 40 05 FA 07 2F 04 C6
0C40 03 AD 00 BD 0C 0A 03 AD 03 79 86 4E 55 4D 42 45
0C50 D2 0B FD 05 C2 05 F2 05 F2 07 F3 04 B6 07 68 05
0C60 0D 00 86 00 2D 07 CD 04 B6 03 9D 03 F7 00 86 FF
```

```
0C70  FF 07 2F 05 1E 0C 08 04 B6 05 0D 06 0B 07 C1 00
0C80  D0 0C 97 04 B6 05 0D 00 86 00 2E 07 C1 05 F2 08
0C90  BE 05 F2 00 BD 0C 71 04 8D 03 AD 00 D0 0C A1 04
0CA0  58 03 79 85 2D 46 49 4E C4 0C 4A 05 C2 06 0B 0B
0CB0  B7 07 84 07 00 04 FA 04 FA 01 96 04 B6 03 D2 00
0CC0  D0 0C CB 04 8D 07 84 08 52 01 96 03 79 87 28 41
0CD0  42 4F 52 54 A9 0C A3 05 C2 0F BE 03 79 85 45 52
0CE0  52 4F D2 0C CD 05 C2 06 9A 04 FA 03 EB 00 D0 0C
0CF0  F3 0C D7 07 84 09 F4 0A 07 0A 68 03 20 20 3F 14

0D00  8C 03 50 06 D1 04 FA 06 C8 04 FA 0F 8D 03 79 83
0D10  4D 49 CE 0C DD 05 C2 04 73 04 73 07 E5 00 D0 0D
0D20  23 04 99 04 8D 03 79 83 49 44 AE 0D 0F 05 C2 0B
0D30  A4 00 86 00 20 00 86 00 5F 0B 4C 04 B6 08 96 08
0D40  62 04 73 07 C1 0B A4 04 99 02 46 0B A4 09 F4 00
0D50  86 00 1F 02 F3 0A 07 08 07 03 79 86 43 52 45 41
0D60  54 C5 0D 27 05 C2 03 3D 07 84 00 86 00 A0 03 F7
0D70  07 D9 06 02 08 BE 0C AB 00 D0 0D 8A 04 8D 08 80
0D80  0D 2D 00 86 00 04 14 8C 08 07 07 84 04 B6 05 0D
0D90  06 8C 04 FA 0D 15 07 68 07 94 04 B6 00 86 00 A0
0DA0  04 E3 07 84 05 FA 07 C1 00 86 00 80 04 E3 08 52
0DB0  07 A0 07 0E 04 FA 05 1E 07 84 07 75 07 A0 03 79
0DC0  C1 BA 0D 5B 05 C2 08 F0 08 AB 07 0E 04 FA 07 00
0DD0  05 1E 0D 64 09 75 00 86 FF FE 06 AF 04 C6 09 51
0DE0  05 C2 03 79 85 21 43 4F 44 C5 0D C0 05 C2 0D 64
0DF0  09 8A 08 52 08 96 08 72 05 1E 07 A0 03 79 88 43

0E00  4F 4E 53 54 41 4E D4 0D E4 05 C2 00 86 05 D6 0D
0E10  EC 03 79 88 56 41 52 49 41 42 4C C5 0D FE 05 C2
0E20  00 86 05 CD 0D EC 03 79 84 55 53 45 D2 0E 13 05
0E30  C2 00 86 05 DF 0D EC 03 79 87 3C 42 55 49 4C 44
0E40  D3 0E 28 05 C2 05 F2 0E 09 03 79 85 44 4F 45 53
0E50  BE 0E 39 05 C2 03 AD 08 52 08 96 05 1E 09 C8 E2
0E60  9A 73 8A 73 4B BA 4B AA 19 19 9B 59 19 8B 59 29
0E70  DC C7 4C 49 54 45 52 41 CC 0E 4B 05 C2 07 1A 04
0E80  FA 00 D0 0E 8B 09 51 00 86 07 A0 03 79 C8 44 4C
0E90  49 54 45 52 41 CC 0E 71 05 C2 07 1A 04 FA 00 D0
0EA0  0E A8 04 99 0E 7B 0E 7B 03 79 86 3F 53 54 41 43
0EB0  CB 0E 8D 05 C2 06 6D 04 FA 04 B6 03 3D 07 E5 05
0EC0  FA 08 BE 00 86 01 00 03 F7 03 3D 07 D9 00 86 00
0ED0  07 08 BE 03 79 89 49 4E 54 45 52 50 52 45 D4 0E
0EE0  AA 05 C2 0C AB 00 D0 0F 05 07 1A 04 FA 07 D9 00
0EF0  D0 0E FB 08 72 07 A0 00 BD 0E FF 08 72 00 A6 0E
```

```
0F00  B3 00 BD 0F 1F 07 84 0C 53 07 2F 04 FA 07 68 00
0F10  D0 0F 19 0E 98 00 BD 0F 1D 04 8D 0E 7B 0E B3 00
0F20  BD 0E E3 03 79 8A 56 4F 43 41 42 55 4C 41 52 D9
0F30  0E D5 05 C2 0E 43 00 86 81 A0 07 A0 07 0E 04 FA
0F40  08 72 07 A0 07 84 06 BE 04 FA 07 A0 06 BE 05 1E
0F50  0E 53 07 75 07 00 05 1E 03 79 C5 46 4F 52 54 C8
0F60  0F 25 0E 5F 0F 52 81 A0 18 BF 00 00 8B 44 45 46
0F70  49 4E 49 54 49 4F 4E D3 0F 5A 05 C2 07 00 04 FA
0F80  07 0E 05 1E 03 79 84 51 55 49 D4 0F 6C 05 C2 05
0F90  F2 06 C8 05 1E 09 67 03 65 05 AB 0A F7 0E E1 07
0FA0  1A 04 FA 03 D2 00 D0 0F B0 0A 68 04 20 20 4F 4B
0FB0  00 BD 0F 97 03 79 85 41 42 4F 52 D4 0F 86 05 C2
0FC0  03 50 09 B2 05 AB 0A 68 1C 31 38 30 32 20 46 49
0FD0  47 2D 46 4F 52 54 48 20 52 30 2E 34 20 20 33 2F
0FE0  31 36 2F 38 31 17 B5 15 AB 06 21 04 B6 15 4D 05
0FF0  1E 15 42 05 1E 0F 62 0F 7A 0F 8D 03 79 C1 BB 0F

1000  B6 05 C2 09 1A 09 51 03 79 09 8A 09 67 03 79 C2
1010  2E A2 0F FD 05 C2 00 86 00 22 07 1A 04 FA 00 D0
1020  10 34 09 51 0A 68 0B B7 07 84 05 0D 07 68 07 94
1030  00 BD 10 3C 0B B7 07 84 09 F4 0A 07 03 79 C9 5B
1040  43 4F 4D 50 49 4C 45 DD 10 0F 05 C2 0C AB 03 D2
1050  05 F2 08 BE 04 8D 08 72 07 A0 03 79 89 49 4D 4D
1060  45 44 49 41 54 C5 10 3E 05 C2 08 52 00 86 00 40
1070  04 E3 03 79 C1 A8 10 5C 05 C2 00 86 00 29 0B B7
1080  03 79 81 B3 10 74 05 D6 00 03 C1 A7 10 82 05 C2
1090  0C AB 03 D2 05 F2 08 BE 04 8D 0E 7B 03 79 86 46
10A0  4F 52 47 45 D4 10 8A 05 C2 07 0E 04 FA 07 00 04
10B0  FA 07 C1 00 86 00 18 08 BE 10 8E 04 B6 06 A6 04
10C0  FA 07 D9 00 86 00 15 08 BE 04 B6 08 80 06 AF 05
10D0  1E 08 62 04 FA 07 00 04 FA 05 1E 03 79 82 2B AD
10E0  10 9E 05 C2 03 EB 00 D0 10 EC 04 12 03 79 83 44
10F0  2B AD 10 DD 05 C2 03 EB 00 D0 10 FE 04 58 03 79

1100  83 41 42 D3 10 EE 05 C2 04 B6 10 E2 03 79 84 44
1110  41 42 D3 11 00 05 C2 04 B6 10 F4 03 79 83 4D 41
1120  D8 11 0E 05 C2 04 73 04 73 07 D9 00 D0 11 31 04
1130  99 04 8D 03 79 82 4D AA 11 1D 05 C2 04 73 04 73
1140  03 24 03 9D 11 06 04 99 11 06 02 78 03 AD 10 F4
1150  03 79 82 4D AF 11 35 05 C2 04 73 03 9D 03 9D 11
1160  15 03 BD 11 06 02 B2 03 AD 03 BD 03 24 10 E2 04
1170  99 03 AD 10 E2 04 99 03 79 81 AA 11 52 05 C2 11
```

```
1180  3A 04 8D 03 79 84 2F 4D 4F C4 11 79 05 C2 03 9D
1190  14 F1 03 AD 11 57 03 79 81 AF 11 85 05 C2 11 8C
11A0  04 99 04 8D 03 79 83 4D 4F C4 11 98 05 C2 11 8C
11B0  04 8D 03 79 85 2A 2F 4D 4F C4 11 A6 05 C2 03 9D
11C0  11 3A 03 AD 11 57 03 79 82 2A AF 11 B4 05 C2 11
11D0  BC 04 99 04 8D 03 79 85 4D 2F 4D 4F C4 11 C8 05
11E0  C2 03 9D 05 F2 03 BD 02 B2 03 AD 04 99 03 9D 02
11F0  B2 03 AD 03 79 83 4D 4F CE 11 D7 11 FD F8 80 B0

1200  F8 00 A0 E0 D0 83 42 59 C5 11 F5 05 C2 18 9B 11
1210  FB 84 42 41 43 CB 12 05 05 C2 07 A0 03 79 C5 42
1220  45 47 49 CE 12 11 05 C2 08 D8 07 84 05 FA 03 79
1230  C5 45 4E 44 49 C6 12 1E 05 C2 08 D8 06 02 09 07
1240  07 84 04 99 05 1E 03 79 C4 54 48 45 CE 12 30 05
1250  C2 12 38 03 79 C2 44 CF 12 48 05 C2 09 51 01 50
1260  07 84 10 86 03 79 C4 4C 4F 4F D0 12 55 05 C2 10
1270  86 09 07 09 51 00 EC 12 18 03 79 C5 2B 4C 4F 4F
1280  D0 12 66 05 C2 10 86 09 07 09 51 01 24 12 18 03
1290  79 C5 55 4E 54 49 CC 12 7B 05 C2 05 FA 09 07 09
12A0  51 00 D0 12 18 03 79 C3 45 4E C4 12 91 05 C2 12
12B0  99 03 79 C5 41 47 41 49 CE 12 A7 05 C2 05 FA 09
12C0  07 09 51 00 BD 12 18 03 79 C6 52 45 50 45 41 D4
12D0  12 B3 05 C2 03 9D 03 9D 12 BB 03 AD 03 AD 06 02
12E0  07 C1 12 38 03 79 C2 49 C6 12 C9 05 C2 09 51 00
12F0  D0 07 84 05 F2 07 A0 06 02 03 79 C4 45 4C 53 C5

1300  12 E6 05 C2 06 02 09 07 09 51 00 BD 07 84 05 F2
1310  07 A0 04 99 06 02 12 38 06 02 03 79 C5 57 48 49
1320  4C C5 12 FB 05 C2 12 EB 07 75 03 79 86 53 50 41
1330  43 45 D3 13 1C 05 C2 05 F2 11 23 08 16 00 D0 13
1340  4B 05 F2 01 50 08 07 00 EC 13 45 03 79 82 3C A3
1350  13 2C 05 C2 0B A4 07 56 05 1E 03 79 82 23 BE 13
1360  4D 05 C2 04 8D 04 8D 07 56 04 FA 0B A4 04 73 07
1370  C1 03 79 84 53 49 47 CE 13 5C 05 C2 07 F3 03 EB
1380  00 D0 13 8A 00 86 00 2D 0B 8C 03 79 81 A3 13 73
1390  05 C2 07 25 04 FA 11 DF 07 F3 00 86 00 09 04 73
13A0  07 D9 00 D0 13 AC 00 86 00 07 03 F7 00 86 00 30
13B0  03 F7 0B 8C 03 79 82 23 D3 13 8C 05 C2 13 90 04
13C0  73 04 73 03 0B 03 D2 00 D0 13 BD 03 79 83 44 2E
13D0  D2 13 B6 05 C2 03 9D 04 99 04 73 11 15 13 52 13
13E0  BB 13 7A 13 61 03 AD 04 73 07 C1 13 35 0A 07 03
13F0  79 82 2E D2 13 CD 05 C2 03 9D 14 F1 03 AD 13 D3
```

```
1400  03 79 82 44 AE 13 F1 05 C2 05 F2 13 D3 08 07 03
1410  79 81 AE 14 02 05 C2 14 F1 14 07 03 79 81 BF 14
1420  11 05 C2 04 FA 14 15 03 79 82 55 AE 14 1D 05 C2
1430  05 F2 14 07 03 79 85 56 4C 49 53 D4 14 29 05 C2
1440  05 AB 00 86 00 80 06 DB 05 1E 07 00 04 FA 04 FA
1450  06 DB 04 FA 06 15 07 E5 00 D0 14 64 05 AB 05 F2
1460  06 DB 05 1E 04 B6 0D 2D 08 07 08 07 08 96 08 62
1470  04 FA 04 B6 03 D2 05 97 03 0B 00 D0 14 50 04 8D
1480  03 79 87 4D 45 53 53 41 47 C5 14 36 05 C2 06 9A
1490  04 FA 00 D0 14 B2 08 16 00 D0 14 AE 00 86 00 04
14A0  06 F2 04 FA 06 45 11 9C 07 C1 15 32 08 07 00 BD
14B0  14 BE 0A 68 07 20 4D 53 47 20 23 20 14 15 03 79
14C0  81 C9 14 82 14 C6 12 19 19 19 42 59 29 02 59 22
14D0  22 DC 84 57 41 52 CD 14 C0 14 DB C0 19 15 84 43
14E0  4F 4C C4 14 D2 14 E7 C0 19 00 84 53 2D 3E C4 14
14F0  DE 14 F3 49 FE 33 FB F8 00 30 FD F8 FF 19 59 19

1500  59 29 DC 86 28 4C 49 4E 45 A9 14 EA 05 C2 03 9D
1510  00 86 00 40 06 39 11 BC 03 AD 06 45 11 7D 03 F7
1520  16 0A 03 F7 00 86 00 40 03 79 85 2E 4C 49 4E C5
1530  15 03 05 C2 15 0C 0A 35 0A 07 03 79 83 55 53 C5
1540  15 2A 05 CD 40 00 84 50 52 45 D6 15 3C 05 CD 40
1550  00 84 2B 42 55 C6 15 46 05 C2 06 39 00 86 00 04
1560  03 F7 03 F7 04 B6 06 2D 07 CD 00 D0 15 72 04 8D
1570  06 21 04 B6 15 4D 04 FA 07 C1 03 79 86 55 50 44
1580  41 54 C5 15 51 05 C2 15 4D 04 FA 04 FA 00 86 80
1590  00 03 0B 15 4D 04 FA 05 1E 03 79 8D 45 4D 50 54
15A0  59 2D 42 55 46 46 45 52 D3 15 7C 05 C2 06 21 06
15B0  2D 04 73 07 C1 0B 6C 03 79 86 42 55 46 46 45 D2
15C0  15 9B 05 C2 15 42 04 FA 04 B6 03 9D 15 58 00 D0
15D0  15 CC 15 42 05 1E 03 BD 04 FA 03 EB 00 D0 15 F2
15E0  03 BD 07 75 03 BD 04 FA 00 86 7F FF 02 F3 05 F2
15F0  16 68 03 BD 05 1E 03 BD 15 4D 05 1E 03 AD 07 75

1600  03 79 85 42 4C 4F 43 CB 15 B9 05 C2 06 F2 04 FA
1610  03 F7 03 9D 15 4D 04 FA 04 B6 04 FA 03 BD 07 C1
1620  04 B6 03 F7 00 D0 16 5A 15 58 03 D2 00 D0 16 42
1630  04 8D 03 BD 15 C2 04 B6 03 BD 05 FA 16 68 06 02
1640  07 C1 04 B6 04 FA 03 BD 07 C1 04 B6 03 F7 03 D2
1650  00 D0 16 28 04 B6 15 4D 05 1E 03 AD 04 8D 07 75
1660  03 79 83 52 2F D7 16 02 05 C2 04 99 00 86 00 FA
1670  11 8C 04 B6 00 86 00 03 07 E5 00 86 00 05 08 BE
1680  04 99 00 86 00 08 11 7D 00 86 00 01 03 F7 00 86
```

```
1690 00 1A 11 8C 07 5F 05 35 05 FA 07 C1 04 99 00 86
16A0 00 40 11 7D 03 F7 07 5F 07 68 05 35 05 F2 07 5F
16B0 07 75 05 35 07 5F 06 39 07 F3 00 D0 16 C4 16 D5
16C0 00 BD 16 C6 17 1F 03 79 0A 42 4C 4F 43 4B 2D 52
16D0 45 41 C4 16 62 16 D7 F8 83 B4 B5 F8 64 A4 F8 74
16E0 A5 E2 9C 73 8C 73 49 B7 09 A7 29 29 09 AC 29 09
16F0 BC 1C 1C 29 09 A8 29 09 B8 29 29 D4 85 02 9F 58

1700 18 27 97 CA 16 FB 87 CA 16 FB E2 60 72 AC F0 BC
1710 DC 0B 42 4C 4F 43 4B 2D 57 52 49 54 C5 16 C8 17
1720 21 F8 83 B4 B5 F8 64 A4 F8 74 A5 E2 9C 73 8C 73
1730 49 B7 09 A7 29 29 09 AC 29 09 BC 1C 1C 29 09 A8
1740 29 09 B8 29 29 48 BF D4 85 00 27 97 CA 17 45 87
1750 CA 17 45 E2 60 72 AC F0 BC DC 84 4C 4F 41 C4 17
1760 11 05 C2 06 C8 04 FA 03 9D 06 D1 04 FA 03 9D 05
1770 F2 06 D1 05 1E 06 45 11 7D 06 C8 05 1E 0E E1 03
1780 AD 06 D1 05 1E 03 AD 06 C8 05 1E 03 79 C3 2D 2D
1790 BE 17 5A 05 C2 09 37 05 F2 06 D1 05 1E 06 45 06
17A0 C8 04 FA 04 73 11 AC 07 C1 06 C8 04 C6 03 79 83
17B0 44 52 B0 17 8D 05 C2 05 F2 06 F2 05 1E 03 79 83
17C0 44 52 B1 17 AF 05 C2 06 45 00 86 00 FA 11 7D 06
17D0 F2 05 1E 03 79 84 4C 49 53 D4 17 BF 05 C2 09 B2
17E0 05 AB 04 B6 06 E5 05 1E 0A 68 06 53 43 52 20 23
17F0 20 14 15 00 86 00 10 05 F2 01 50 05 AB 14 C4 00

1800 86 00 03 13 F6 08 07 14 C4 06 E5 04 FA 15 32 05
1810 97 00 D0 18 17 03 89 00 EC 17 FB 05 AB 03 79 85
1820 49 4E 44 45 D8 17 D5 05 C2 05 AB 07 68 04 99 01
1830 50 05 AB 14 C4 00 86 00 03 13 F6 08 07 05 F2 14
1840 C4 15 32 05 97 00 D0 18 4B 03 89 00 EC 18 31 03
1850 79 85 54 52 49 41 C4 18 1F 05 C2 05 AB 00 86 00
1860 03 11 9C 00 86 00 03 11 7D 00 86 00 03 04 73 03
1870 F7 04 99 01 50 05 AB 14 C4 17 DC 05 97 00 D0 18
1880 83 03 89 00 EC 18 75 05 AB 00 86 00 0F 14 8C 05
1890 AB 03 79 85 46 4C 55 53 C8 18 51 05 C2 06 2D 06
18A0 21 07 C1 06 39 00 86 00 04 03 F7 11 9C 05 F2 01
18B0 50 00 86 7F FF 15 C2 04 8D 00 EC 18 B1 03 79 84
18C0 54 41 53 CB 18 93 05 C2 03 79 00 00 00 00 00 00
18D0 00 00 00 00 00 00 00 00 00 00 00 00 00 00 00 00
18E0 00 00 00 00 00 00 00 00 00 00 00 00 00 00 00 00
18F0 00 00 00 00 00 00 00 00 00 00 00 00 00 00 00 00

1900 F8 00 B7 F8 6A A7 F8 0F B8 F8 68 A8 47 58 18 47
```

```
1910 58 F8 16 30 17 F8 10 AF F8 00 B7 F8 6E A7 47 BD
1920 B8 07 AD A8 F8 6A A7 47 58 18 2F 8F 3A 27 F8 00
1930 BC F8 92 AC F8 C0 AA F8 0F BA C0 03 67 C4 00 00
1940 00 00 00 00 00 00 00 00 00 00 00 00 00 00 00 00
1950 00 00 00 00 00 00 00 00 00 00 00 00 00 00 00 00
1960 00 00 00 00 00 00 00 00 00 00 00 00 00 00 00 00
1970 00 00 00 00 00 00 00 00 00 00 00 00 00 00 00 00
1980 00 00 00 00 00 00 00 00 00 00 00 00 00 00 00 00
1990 00 00 00 00 00 00 00 00 00 00 00 00 00 00 00 00
19A0 00 00 00 00 00 00 00 00 00 00 00 00 00 00 00 00
19B0 00 00 00 00 00 00 00 00 00 00 00 00 00 00 00 00
19C0 00 00 00 00 00 00 00 00 00 00 00 00 00 00 00 00
19D0 00 00 00 00 00 00 00 00 00 00 00 00 00 00 00 00
19E0 00 00 00 00 00 00 00 00 00 00 00 00 00 00 00 00
19F0 00 00 00 00 00 00 00 00 00 00 00 00 00 00 00 00

1A00 00 00 00 00 00 00 00 00 00 00 00 00 00 00 00 00
1A10 00 00 00 00 00 00 00 00 00 00 00 00 00 00 00 00
1A20 00 00 00 00 00 00 00 00 00 00 00 00 00 00 00 00
1A30 00 00 00 00 00 00 00 00 00 00 00 00 00 00 00 00
1A40 00 00 00 00 00 00 00 00 00 00 00 00 00 00 00 00
1A50 00 00 00 00 00 00 00 00 00 00 00 00 00 00 00 00
1A60 00 00 00 00 00 00 00 00 00 00 00 00 00 00 00 00
1A70 00 00 00 00 00 00 00 00 00 00 00 00 00 00 00 00
1A80 00 00 00 00 00 00 00 00 00 00 00 00 00 00 00 00
1A90 00 00 00 00 00 00 00 00 00 00 00 00 00 00 00 00
1AA0 00 00 00 00 00 00 00 00 00 00 00 00 00 00 00 00
1AB0 00 00 00 00 00 00 00 00 00 00 00 00 00 00 00 00
1AC0 00 00 00 00 00 00 00 00 00 00 00 00 00 00 00 00
1AD0 00 00 00 00 00 00 00 00 00 00 00 00 00 00 00 00
1AE0 00 00 00 00 00 00 00 00 00 00 00 00 00 00 00 00
1AF0 00 00 00 00 00 00 00 00 00 00 00 00 00 00 00 00

1B00 00 00 00 00 00 00 00 00 00 00 00 00 00 00 00 00
1B10 00 00 00 00 00 00 00 00 00 00 00 00 00 00 00 00
1B20 00 00 00 00 00 00 00 00 00 00 00 00 00 00 00 00
1B30 00 00 00 00 00 00 00 00 00 00 00 00 00 00 00 00
1B40 00 00 00 00 00 00 00 00 00 00 00 00 00 00 00 00
1B50 00 00 00 00 00 00 00 00 00 00 00 00 00 00 00 00
1B60 00 00 00 00 00 00 00 00 00 00 00 00 00 00 00 00
1B70 00 00 00 00 00 00 00 00 00 00 00 00 00 00 00 00
1B80 00 00 00 00 00 00 00 00 00 00 00 00 00 00 00 00
1B90 00 00 00 00 00 00 00 00 00 00 00 00 00 00 00 00
```

```
1BA0  00 00 00 00 00 00 00 00 00 00 00 00 00 00 00 00
1BB0  00 00 00 00 00 00 00 00 00 00 00 00 00 00 00 00
1BC0  00 00 00 00 00 00 00 00 00 00 00 00 00 00 00 00
1BD0  00 00 00 00 00 00 00 00 00 00 00 00 00 00 00 00
1BE0  00 00 00 00 00 00 00 00 00 00 00 00 00 00 00 00
1BF0  00 00 00 00 00 00 00 00 00 00 00 00 00 00 00 00

1C00  00 00 00 00 00 00 00 00 00 00 00 00 00 00 00 00
1C10  00 00 00 00 00 00 00 00 00 00 00 00 00 00 00 00
1C20  00 00 00 00 00 00 00 00 00 00 00 00 00 00 00 00
1C30  00 00 00 00 00 00 00 00 00 00 00 00 00 00 00 00
1C40  00 00 00 00 00 00 00 00 00 00 00 00 00 00 00 00
1C50  00 00 00 00 00 00 00 00 00 00 00 00 00 00 00 00
1C60  00 00 00 00 00 00 00 00 00 00 00 00 00 00 00 00
1C70  00 00 00 00 00 00 00 00 00 00 00 00 00 00 00 00
1C80  00 00 00 00 00 00 00 00 00 00 00 00 00 00 00 00
1C90  00 00 00 00 00 00 00 00 00 00 00 00 00 00 00 00
1CA0  00 00 00 00 00 00 00 00 00 00 00 00 00 00 00 00
1CB0  00 00 00 00 00 00 00 00 00 00 00 00 00 00 00 00
1CC0  00 00 00 00 00 00 00 00 00 00 00 00 00 00 00 00
1CD0  00 00 00 00 00 00 00 00 00 00 00 00 00 00 00 00
1CE0  00 00 00 00 00 00 00 00 00 00 00 00 00 00 00 00
1CF0  00 00 00 00 00 00 00 00 00 00 00 00 00 00 00 00

1D00  00 00 00 00 00 00 00 00 00 00 00 00 00 00 00 00
1D10  00 00 00 00 00 00 00 00 00 00 00 00 00 00 00 00
1D20  00 00 00 00 00 00 00 00 00 00 00 00 00 00 00 00
1D30  00 00 00 00 00 00 00 00 00 00 00 00 00 00 00 00
1D40  00 00 00 00 00 00 00 00 00 00 00 00 00 00 00 00
1D50  00 00 00 00 00 00 00 00 00 00 00 00 00 00 00 00
1D60  00 00 00 00 00 00 00 00 00 00 00 00 00 00 00 00
1D70  00 00 00 00 00 00 00 00 00 00 00 00 00 00 00 00
1D80  00 00 00 00 00 00 00 00 00 00 00 00 00 00 00 00
1D90  00 00 00 00 00 00 00 00 00 00 00 00 00 00 00 00
1DA0  00 00 00 00 00 00 00 00 00 00 00 00 00 00 00 00
1DB0  00 00 00 00 00 00 00 00 00 00 00 00 00 00 00 00
1DC0  00 00 00 00 00 00 00 00 00 00 00 00 00 00 00 00
1DD0  00 00 00 00 00 00 00 00 00 00 00 00 00 00 00 00
1DE0  00 00 00 00 00 00 00 00 00 00 00 00 00 00 00 00
1DF0  00 00 00 00 00 00 00 00 00 00 00 00 00 00 00 00

1E00  00 00 00 00 00 00 00 00 00 00 00 00 00 00 00 00
1E10  00 00 00 00 00 00 00 00 00 00 00 00 00 00 00 00
```

```
1E20 00 00 00 00 00 00 00 00 00 00 00 00 00 00 00 00
1E30 00 00 00 00 00 00 00 00 00 00 00 00 00 00 00 00
1E40 00 00 00 00 00 00 00 00 00 00 00 00 00 00 00 00
1E50 00 00 00 00 00 00 00 00 00 00 00 00 00 00 00 00
1E60 00 00 00 00 00 00 00 00 00 00 00 00 00 00 00 00
1E70 00 00 00 00 00 00 00 00 00 00 00 00 00 00 00 00
1E80 00 00 00 00 00 00 00 00 00 00 00 00 00 00 00 00
1E90 00 00 00 00 00 00 00 00 00 00 00 00 00 00 00 00
1EA0 00 00 00 00 00 00 00 00 00 00 00 00 00 00 00 00
1EB0 00 00 00 00 00 00 00 00 00 00 00 00 00 00 00 00
1EC0 00 00 00 00 00 00 00 00 00 00 00 00 00 00 00 00
1ED0 00 00 00 00 00 00 00 00 00 00 00 00 00 00 00 00
1EE0 00 00 00 00 00 00 00 00 00 00 00 00 00 00 00 00
1EF0 00 00 00 00 00 00 00 00 00 00 00 00 00 00 00 00

1F00 00 00 00 00 00 00 00 00 00 00 00 00 00 00 00 00
1F10 00 00 00 00 00 00 00 00 00 00 00 00 00 00 00 00
1F20 00 00 00 00 00 00 00 00 00 00 00 00 00 00 00 00
1F30 00 00 00 00 00 00 00 00 00 00 00 00 00 00 00 00
1F40 00 00 00 00 00 00 00 00 00 00 00 00 00 00 00 00
1F50 00 00 00 00 00 00 00 00 00 00 00 00 00 00 00 00
1F60 00 00 00 00 00 00 00 00 00 00 00 00 00 00 00 00
1F70 00 00 00 00 00 00 00 00 00 00 00 00 00 00 00 00
1F80 00 00 00 00 00 00 00 00 00 00 00 00 00 00 00 00
1F90 00 00 00 00 00 00 00 00 00 00 00 00 00 00 00 00
1FA0 00 00 00 00 00 00 00 00 00 00 00 00 00 00 00 00
1FB0 00 00 00 00 00 00 00 00 00 00 00 00 00 00 00 00
1FC0 00 00 00 00 00 00 00 00 00 00 00 00 00 00 00 00
1FD0 00 00 00 00 00 00 00 00 00 00 00 00 00 00 00 00
1FE0 00 00 00 00 00 00 00 00 00 00 00 00 00 00 00 00
1FF0 00 00 00 00 00 00 00 00 00 00 00 00 00 00 00 00
```

The Lattice FPGA Board connections – top view:

D11 - Power ON   J5 USB   exaleys.com   ICE40-HX8k Breakout Board

Addresses:
LEDs
61440
OUT 1
61442
OUT 2
61443
IN 1
61444
IN 2
61445
Reset Switch
J2
39_GND
35_D16

J4

GND_40		39_GND	
023 B2_38		37_B1	I24
022 C2_36		35_C1	I23
021 D2_34		33_D1	I22
GND_32		31_GND	
020 F1_30		29_E2	I21
017 G1_28		27_F2	I20
016 H1_26		25_62	I17
GND_24		23_GND	
CLK J3_22		21_H2	I16
015 J1_20		19_J2	I15
014 K1_18		17_K3	I14
GND_16		15_GND	
013 L1_14		13_L3	I13
012 M1_12		11_M2	I12
011 N2_10		09_N3	I11
GND_08		07_GND	
010 P2_06		05_P1	I10
R1_04		03_33	
I03_02		01_33	

J3

GND_40		39_GND	
T2_38		37_T1	
T3_36		35_R2	
R4_34		33_R3	
GND_32		31_GND	
R5_30		29_I5	
R6_28		27_I8	
T8_26		25_I7	
GND_24		23_GND	
R9_22		21_I8	
P9_20		19_P8	
R10_18		17_I10	
GND_16		15_GND	
P10_14		13_I11	
027 M11_12		11_N10	
026 P13_10		09_N12	I27
GND_08		07_GND	
025 T14_06		05_I13	I28
024 T16_04		03_I15	I25
I02_02		01_R16	

J1

GND_40		39_GND
A1_38		37_A2
B3_36		35_B4
C3_34		33_B5
GND_32		31_GND
C4_30		29_A5
C5_28		27_B6
C6_26		25_A6
GND_24		23_GND
C7_22		21_B7
A7_20		19_B8
B9_18		17_A9
GND_16		15_GND
C9_14		13_A10
B10_12		11_A11
B11_10		09_B12
GND_08		07_GND
B14_06		05_B13
B15_04		03_A15
I08_02		01_A16

J2

GND_40		39_GND RES
B16_38		37_C16
D14_36		35_D16 RES
D15_34		33_E16
GND_32		31_GND
E14_30		29_F16
F15_28		27_G16
G15_26		25_H16
GND_24		23_GND
H14_22		21_J15
F14_20		19_G14
J14_18		17_K14
GND_16		15_GND
K16_14		13_K15
L16_12		11_M16
M16_10		09_N16
GND_08		07_GND
P15_06		05_P16
R15_04		03_12
I01_02		01_12

LEDs 2 3 4 5 6 7 8 9

LATTICE

IO Connections OUT 1, OUT 2, IN 1 IN 2; RESET is on J2 Pin 35 to Pin 39

Left (J4)				Right (J3)			
GND_40	● ●	39_GND		GND_40	● ●	39_GND	
O23 B2_38	● ●	37_B1	I24	T2_38	● ●	37_T1	
O22 C2_36	● ●	35_C1	I23	T3_36	● ●	35_R2	
O21 D2_34	● ●	33_D1	I22	R4_34	● ●	33_R3	
GND_32	● ●	31_GND		GND_32	● ●	31_GND	
O20 F1_30	● ●	29_E2	I21	R5_30	● ●	29_T5	
O17 G1_28	● ●	27_F2	I20	R6_28	● ●	27_T6	
O16 H1_26	● ●	25_G2	I17	T8_26	● ●	25_T7	
GND_24	● ●	23_GND		GND_24	● ●	23_GND	
CLK J3_22	● ●	21_H2	I16	R9_22	● ●	21_T9	
O15 J1_20	● ●	19_J2	I15	P9_20	● ●	19_P8	
O14 K1_18	● ●	17_K3	I14	R10_18	● ●	17_T10	
GND_16	● ●	15_GND		GND_16	● ●	15_GND	
O13 L1_14	● ●	13_L3	I13	P10_14	● ●	13_T11	
O12 M1_12	● ●	11_M2	I12	O27 M11_12	● ●	11_N10	
O11 N2_10	● ●	09_N3	I11	O26 P13_10	● ●	09_N12	I27
GND_08	● ●	07_GND		GND_08	● ●	07_GND	
O10 P2_06	● ●	05_P1	I10	O25 T14_06	● ●	05_T13	I26
R1_04	● ●	03_3	3	O24 T16_04	● ●	03_T15	I25
I03_02	● ●	01_3	3	I02_02	● ●	01_R16	

J4   J3

####

Dr. Chen-Hanson Ting

Introduction:
Retired chemist-turned-engineer

How long have you been interested in Forth:
32 years

Bio:

PhD in chemistry, University of Chicago, 1965.
Professor of chemistry in Taiwan until 1975.

Firmware engineer in Silicon Valley until retirement in 2000. Still actively composing Forth Haikus.

Custodian of the eForth systems since 1990,
still maintaining eForth systems for Arduino, MSP430, and various ARM microcontrollers.

Author of eP8, eP16, eP24, and eP32 microcontrollers in VHDL, which were implemented on several FPGA chips.

Offete Enterprises, started in 1975, and is now formally closed.
However, Dr. Ting can still be contacted
through email chenhting@yahoo.com.tw

(source www.forth.org/whoswho.html#chting)

Exeter UK - ExMark - Juergen Pintaske - June 2020

www.ingramcontent.com/pod-product-compliance
Lightning Source LLC
LaVergne TN
LVHW051236050326
832903LV00028B/2435